World War II

Remembered

H.R.H. PRINCE PHILIP - WORLD WAR II

Prince Philip left Dartmouth, where he had been the outstanding cadet of his term winning the King's Dirk, in 1940, becoming a Midshipman in the battleship RAMILLIES, a unit of the Mediterranean Fleet. In January 1941, he joined the VALIANT, and in charge of a section of searchlights, illuminated the Italian cruiser force that his ship, together with the WARSPITE and the BARHAM, sank in the night action off Cape Matapan, being mentioned in his dispatches by the Commander-in-Chief. As hostilities in Europe ceased, he was the First Lieutenant in the destroyer WHELP which then went East to join the British Pacific Fleet, and was present at the surrender of the Japanese Fleet in Tokyo Bay on 2 September 1945.

BUCKINGHAM PALACE.

The generation which took part in the Second World War is thinning out rapidly and their children and grandchildren will soon no longer get firsthand accounts of that extraordinary bout of madness that gripped such a large part of the world 50 years ago. Fighting of one kind or another took place in almost every country in existence at the time, from huge armoured clashes deep in the Soviet Union to the small, but equally fierce, campaigns of the resistance fighters in occupied countries.

Most of the people of Britain and Europe were inevitably caught up in the struggle against Germany and Italy, but it should never be forgotten that in North Africa and the Far East men and women from all over, what was then, the British Empire were fighting side by side and with our North American Allies against the Japanese.

Many photographs and paintings were made during the First World War, but the equipment was fairly primitive. In contrast, the Second World War was covered in the greatest detail by the media and official war artists. I am sure that this collection will bring back many memories to those who were there and I hope that it will give a flavour of those events, great and small, to the younger and future generations.

Battles were fought on and under all the oceans and for the first time in maritime history, naval aviation decided the outcome of encounters between surface fleets. Both the Royal and Merchant Navies suffered many casualties in these operations, so I am delighted that the proceeds from the sale of this book will go to King George's Fund for Sailors, whose main purpose is to provide support for all distressed seafarers and their dependents.

KING GEORGE'S FUND FOR SAILORS gratefully acknowledges the generosity and interest of the following organisations who made the publication of *World War II Remembered* possible.

A

Adwest Group plc	46
Allied Lyone PLC	61
Associated British Ports Holding PLC	83
Associated Fisheries PLC	29
Associated Newspapers Holdings Ltd	31
Australia & New Zealand Banking Grp Ltd	101
Avon Rubber PLC	12
AXA Equity & Law Life Assurance Society	77

B

Barclays Bank PLC	16
Baring Brothers & Co Limited	49
Barr & Stroud Ltd	68
B.A.T Industries PLC	80
Bentalls Public Limited Company	85
Blackwells of Oxford	79
The Boots Company PLC	56
BPB Industries plc	87
British Aerospace plc	88
British Airways Plc	112
British Engines Ltd	91
British Telecommunications PLC	57
David Brown Group PLC	81

C

Cadbury Schweppes PLC	99
Calor Group PLC	84
Cazenove & Co	103
Charter plc	105
Chelsea Building Society	53
Constantine Group	42
Corporation of London - End pages	
Courage Charitable Trust	28
Cox's & King's Branch, Lloyds Bank	95

D

Alfred Dunhill Ltd	37

E

Enterprise Oil plc	106
Express Dairy Ltd	67

F

Fina plc	48
Fine Art Developments p.l.c.	77
Robert Fleming Holdings Ltd	89
Forte Plc	18
FR Group plc	78

G

GEC-Marconi	43
Geest PLC	91
Sir Alexander Gibbs & Partners Ltd	81
GKN PLC	86
Greycoat PLC	14
Guardian Royal Exchange plc	40

H

Halifax Building Society	71
Hambros PLC	25
Harrisons (Clyde) Ltd	32
Harrisons & Crosfield plc	66
Hillsdown Holdings plc	64
Healey & Baker	47
The Jane Hodge Foundation	46
Holman, Fenwick & Willan	22
HP Foods Ltd	63
Hunting Engineering Ltd	19

I

Imperial Chemical Industries PLC	39
Imperial Tobacco Ltd	65
Industria Engineering Products Ltd	20
The Institute of London Underwriters	39
The Institute of Marine Engineers	44

K

Kidde-Graviner Ltd	34

L

Laings Charitable Trust	82
Land Rover Ltd	110 & 111
Land Securities PLC	15
Lazard Brothers & Co Ltd	59
Lombard North Central PLC	45
London Transport	58
Low & Bonar plc	72

M

Macmillan Publishers Ltd	100
MacTaggart Scott & Co Ltd	41
The Maersk Company Limited	94
J Marr Ltd	29
Bernard Matthews P.L.C.	73
Mobil Shipping Ltd	32
Wm Morrison Supermarket plc	102

N

National Westminster Bank Plc	51
Nicholson Leslie Ltd	39

P

The Peninsular & Oriental Steam Navigation Company Limited	9
Perkins Engines (Shrewsbury) Ltd	92
Portals Group plc	62
Port of Felixstowe	97
Port of London Authority	50
Portsmouth & Sunderland Newspapers plc	10

Provident Mutual Life Assurance Assoc	50

R

Racal Electronics Plc	70
The Rank Organisation PLC	27
The Reader's Digest Trust	36
Reckitt & Colman plc	74
Reuters Holding PLC	108
RHP Bearings Ltd	70
Rolls-Royce plc	24
Ropner plc	32
Royal Mint	107
Royal Ordnance Plc	58
Rutland Trust plc	109

S

Saatchi & Saatchi Advertising Ltd	35
J Sainsbury plc	30
Robin Salvesen	90
Scottish Fisheries Museum Trust Ltd	29
Scottish Hydro-Electric plc	76
Shell International Petroleum Company Ltd	23
Shepherd Building Group Ltd	60
Singer & Friedlander Ltd	21
W H Smith Group PLC	8
Spillers Foods Ltd	98
Bernard Sunley Charitable Fdn	69
John Swire & Sons Ltd	13

T

Texaco Ltd	54
TI Group plc	77
TNT Express (UK) Ltd	109
Tomkins PLC	33
Trago Mills Ltd	12
Tyne Tees Television	52

U

Unigate PLC	26
Unilever PLC	38

V

Vaux Group plc	55
Vickers P.L.C.	75
VSEL	11

W

Wassall PLC	104
Westminster Dredging Co Ltd	96
Garfield Weston Foundation	17

Y

Young & Co's Brewery PLC	93

Published by: SEAGULL S.A. P O Box 122, Helvetia Court, South Esplanade, St Peters Port, Guernsey Channel Islands GY1 4EE.

Typesetting: Saffron Graphics Ltd, King's Exchange, 8A Tileyard Road, York Way, London N7 9AH, England.

Origination & Colour Separation: London Scanning Ltd, London, England.

Printed and bound by: Tien Wah Press (PTE.) Ltd. (Singapore).

Distributed by: King George's Fund for Sailors. 8 Hatherley Street, London SW1P 2YY, England. (Registered Charity No. 226446)

CONTENTS

KGFS

Patron HER MAJESTY THE QUEEN

ACKNOWLEDGMENTS

WORLD WAR II REMEMBERED was always going to be a formidable
undertaking. To cover six of the most crucial and climactic years in
human history and not only report them factually, but to try and
relay something of the atmosphere of those dramatic, dangerous yet
stimulating times - all in a volume of practical proportions, and
with the accent on the visual, could never be particularly easy.

Yet to mark the 50th Anniversary of that war's end, on the last major
occasion on which it will be able to be recalled by the living,
either adults or children at the time, was a challenge that a great
national Fund such as ours could not ignore - so many of our
beneficiaries having paid such a high price in its cause.

Fortunately, as indeed during the war itself, generous aid and
co-operation rallied round. Dr Alan Borg's Imperial War Museum
provided much of the photographic and art material and we would like
to specially single out, from all the helpful staff there, Pauline
Allwright, Photographic Services Administrator, Angela Weight, Keeper
of the Department of Art, Hilary Roberts, Head of Collections
Department, and John Delaney. The National Maritime Museum also
rendered indespensable help, through Christopher Gray and Robert Todd
of the Picture Library; and our thanks also goes to the Fleet Air
Arm Museum at Yeovilton and the RAF Museum at Hendon.

And then there are today's artists, to whom we owe such a deep debt
of gratitude for making some of the most famous episodes in this
great conflict live so vividly in these ages - Terence Cuneo, Frank
Wootton, Michael Turner, Robert Taylor, Mrs Betty Hamilton for the
fine naval works of her late husband, John Hamilton, Pat Barnard's
Military Gallery in Bath, Alan Fearney, Ronald Wong, David Shepherd
and the Parker Gallery and the Army Benevolent Fund - all of whom
loaned the copyrights of their splendidly evocative paintings. For
other photographs we thank Richard Wilson; and for invaluable
material on the Home Front, Macmillan Publishers; and Alan Symes of
the Central Office of Information. Indeed there are also many others
in Regimental Museums and Service Associations across the country,
too numerous to mention, whose help is most appreciated.

We hope that you will agree that the result, edited like our last
book by Avril Evans, not only portrays the epic and the ordinary of
warfare, but some of the nostalgia and flavour of everyday life in
those times.

Captain M J Appleton RN
Director General
King George's Fund for Sailors

KING GEORGE'S FUND·FOR SAILORS

Registered Charity No. 226446

From
Chairman of the General Council
Admiral SIR BRIAN BROWN, KCB, CBE

8, Hatherley Street,

London SW1P 2YY

For the past seventy eight years King George's Fund for Sailors (KGFS) has been raising and distributing funds to help seafarers of the Royal Navy, the Royal Marines, the Merchant Navy and the Fishing Fleets and their dependants who are in need. Fifty years ago at the end of World War II no fewer than one million sailors were at sea in the service of this country and more than eighty five thousand had been killed or injured. Many of those sailors families were left to fend for themselves and increasing numbers are now in need of help.

Through the generosity of the publishers Messrs Seagull and the Companies and Organisations who have sponsored the pages of this book, all the proceeds from its sale come to KGFS.

Since 1917, the year of our foundation, KGFS has distributed over £25 million and year on year the level of our annual grants total increases. Over the last five years the level of the Fund's annual grants has risen by 52% and in 1994 the total was £2.1/2 million. In this World War II anniversary year it is expected to exceed that figure by a substantial amount.

Our aim is to provide help to seafarers and their families wherever and whenever help is needed. By buying this book you help us to continue to do this.

Thank you for your support and to all those who have contributed to the publication of this book.

Brian Brown

"THIS COUNTRY IS AT WAR … "

The 3rd of September 1939 was a bright, sunny Sunday morning with the usual preoccupation with the papers and their account of the crisis in Europe that many believed, and all hoped, would never actually develop into another war. As thoughts turned to the Sunday roast gently wafting from the kitchen and afternoon plans were laid to take advantage of the fine weather, the melodious thirties tune stopped abruptly on the 'wireless' –

"Here is an announcement: at 11.15, that is in about two minutes, the Prime Minister will broadcast to the nation – please stand by".

There was a peal of bells, which only heightened the suspenseful silence as fixed gazes concentrated on the set for what seemed an interminable interval, then came: "This is London. You will now hear a statement by the Prime Minister, the Right Honourable Neville Chamberlain, MP …"

Into farflung Hebridean island and Channel naval base, a sombre, slow voice intoned: "I am speaking to you from the Cabinet Room at 10 Downing Street. This morning, the British Ambassador in Berlin handed the German Government the Final Note stating that unless we heard from them by eleven o'clock that they were prepared, at once, to withdraw their troops from Poland, a state of war would exist between us. (There was the briefest pause, heavy with portent) I have to tell you that no such undertaking has been received, and that consequently, this country is at war with Germany …"

There was another peal of bells, then the spontaneous outbursts across the nation, of concern, surprise, anger, macho-patriotism and even relief for those who'd worried for too long were cut short by "sshh's" as the announcer started reading a series of 'Government Notices' – about places of entertainment being closed – what people should do in the event of a snap air raid – how gas masks should *always* be carried …

When it was finished, the very English priorities of the Sunday joint and afternoon outing were suddenly superseded by the realisation that nothing was going to stay the same.

W H SMITH GROUP PLC

Rawalpindi

'NO SURRENDER' – RAWALPINDI

On 3 September 1939, the 368 ships of P&O and its subsidiary companies were scattered, as usual, round the globe.

On 23 November, three months after being requisitioned as an armed merchant cruiser, the P&O liner *Rawalpindi* was on patrol between Iceland and the Faeroe Islands. By mid-afternoon, dusk was already coming on, with mist over the sea making visibility still poorer, when a very large, vague shape was seen approaching. For some minutes it was difficult to identify: then the men in *Rawalpindi* realised they were about to face the battlecruiser *Scharnhorst*. Ten years younger than *Rawalpindi*, her armament included nine 11-inch and twelve 5.9 inch guns, and she was making the German Navy's first attempt to break out into the Atlantic. To try and stop her with *Rawalpindi* would be rather like bicycling towards a tank. Captain E C Kennedy, RN, commanding *Rawalpindi*, signalled the sighting to the Home Fleet in Scapa Flow, turned his vessel, and made for the shelter of a fog bank. First by light and then by a shot across the bows, *Scharnhorst*, thinking *Rawalpindi* was an unarmed merchant

ship, signalled her to heave to; and at that moment Kennedy sighted *Gneisenau*. The fog bank was unattainable. A third challenge came from *Scharnhorst*, and rather than surrender, Kennedy pedalled his metaphorical bicycle against both enemy vessels, opening fire with his antique guns. Very quickly, *Rawalpindi* scored at least one hit on *Scharnhorst*. However, both the great warships hit the old liner time after time, and 14 minutes after the first shot she was a dead ship. 'They must have known as they sighted the enemy that there was no chance for them,' said Prime Minister Chamberlain to the House of Commons a few days later, 'but they had no thought of surrender. They fought their guns till they could be fought no more …'.

The P&O Group lost 179 ships during the War. On the 50th Anniversary of the D-Day landings, during which thirteen P&O ships had taken part, the Company's flagship *Canberra* had the honour of taking some 600 veterans on a return to the Normandy beaches.

THE PENINSULAR AND ORIENTAL STEAM NAVIGATION COMPANY

PORTSMOUTH...... PREPARATION FOR THE GERMAN INVASION, SEPTEMBER 1939

SUNDERLAND...... UNDERCARRIAGE OF GERMAN BOMBER BEING INSPECTED AFTER IT HAD BEEN BROUGHT DOWN, SEPTEMBER 7, 1940

THE BATTLE OF THE RIVER PLATE

The German pocket battleship, ADMIRAL GRAF SPEE, which had been attacking Allied shipping shortly after the outbreak of World War II, sank two British merchant ships on the 2nd and 3rd December 1939, near the Cape route in the South Atlantic and then proceeded west to the busy shipping route off South America. Before the two ships sank, however, they were able to report the attacks and give their positions.

Commodore H. H. Harwood, flying his pennant in HMS AJAX, received news of the sinkings as he sailed north from the Falkland Islands, with HMS Exeter and HMNZS ACHILLES and decided to concentrate his force in an area off the River Plate estuary. The force was divided into two divisions, the AJAX and ACHILLES in one and HMS EXETER in the other, the plan was that, on meeting the enemy, they would attack from different directions.

At about 0600 on 13th December 1939, the GRAF SPEE sighted the three British cruisers and went to action stations; shortly afterwards, HMS EXETER reported her to be in sight. A few minutes later, the GRAF SPEE opened fire with her main armament on to the Exeter and with her secondary armament on to the AJAX and ACHILLES. HMS EXETER immediately altered course to the westward and opened fire, whilst AJAX and ACHILLES made for the other side of the GRAF SPEE, opening fire soon after. Within an hour, HMS EXETER had been hit several times, her forward turrets and bridge were out of action and very serious fires had started on board. However, EXETER had managed to hit the GRAF SPEE a number of times, before being forced to break off the action at about 0730 and had also made a determined but unsuccessful torpedo attack on the enemy. Meanwhile, the AJAX and ACHILLES

had closed with the Graf Spee and scored a considerable number of hits. AJAX fired her torpedoes, but they were avoided by the enemy. Both AJAX and ACHILLES were damaged and when AJAX'S after turrets were put out of action at 0740, Commodore Harwood decided to break off the action and shadow the German Ship. HMS EXETER with a list to starboard and down by the bows, was ordered to return to the Falklands for repairs.

The Captain of the GRAF SPEE, Captain Langsdorff, decided that, in view of the severe damage to his ship and the great distance from his home bases, he would make for Montevideo and get permission from the Uruguayan Government to stay there long enough to make the necessary repairs to his ship. Early in the morning of 14th December, the GRAF SPEE anchored off Montevideo and AJAX and ACHILLES patrolled outside the harbour, in international waters. Additional support was on the way; HMS CUMBERLAND from the Falklands and HMS ARK ROYAL, HMS REVENGE and three cruisers were steaming down from the north. Captain Langsdorff had hoped that the Uruguayan Government would allow him to stay in harbour longer than the 72 hours laid down by international law. In spite of strong pressure from the German Ambassador, this the Uruguayan Government refused to allow. The necessary repairs could not be carried out within the stipulated time limit and on Sunday evening the 17th December 1939, the GRAF SPEE put to sea. Shortly after 2000, two explosions shook the ship and a flash of flame leapt skywards as she blew herself up. The GRAF SPEE had been scuttled by her Commander on the express orders of Hitler; Captain Langsdorff committing suicide ashore on his ship's battle ensign.

COMING TO TERMS WITH WAR

During the crisis in Czechoslovakia, in September 1938, more than 38 million gas masks were issued throughout Britain (that particular crisis also produced many sudden marriages and record sales of readymade wills). This vast exercise, all of it by volunteers, was the first example of the communal effort that was to become so widespread on the Home Front in so many aspects of the war.

The masks themselves were clammy, and smelt of rubber and disinfectant and particularly unpleasant for people with breathing difficulties and imagined or real claustrophobia; but with the still visible human evidence in the community of those who'd suffered gas attacks in the First World War, their acceptance was universal – and nearly so was also the concentration of the population's mind that they were approaching a war-footing, with real personal dangers for them. Children's masks were given the appealing touch of a Mickey Mouse face and there was a special air-tight 'gas helmet' for babies.

Exercises were undertaken by local Civil Defence authorities who picked their way through mythical post-air raid debris to locate dozens of mustard gas 'casualties', who were rushed to the municipal swimming pool Emergency Aid Centre, where a gallery full of civic dignitaries and official observers saw nurses compulsorily strip all of them, including those who'd failed to wear the recommended bathing costumes, of their 'contaminated' clothing.

At least the protection offered was universal, unlike the Anderson Shelter, consisting of fourteen sheets of corrugated iron embedded four feet into the earth; where only the 27 per cent of the population with gardens could benefit and only those with an annual income of less than £250 per year were exempt from the £7 fee.

And out of town the inconveniences of war made their presence felt, too. road signs were painted out to confuse any invader or spy: And they did confuse - most of the indigeonous population who ventured beyond familiar haunts, many a petrol allowance being wasted on a journey to nowhere, Barbed wire blossomed on beaches, though some took it in their stride!

I.W.M

AVON RUBBER PLC

TRAGO MILLS LIMITED

NARVIK

On the night of 8-9th April 1940, the Admiralty received RAF intelligence that major naval German units had sailed from their bases and assumed that a North Atlantic sweep was about to be made – totally failing to comprehend that the Germans were in the process of invading Norway; even though just such an invasion was being planned by the Allies for a fortnight later. On the 9th of April ten large German destroyers carrying 2000 mountain troops arrived off Narvik, sank two Norwegian warships at anchor, and landed them. The destroyers, which had used up all their fuel on the long voyage from home, had to await the arrival of a tanker; and on the same day Captain Warburton-Lee with a flotilla of five Royal Navy destroyers asked the Norwegian pilots, at the entrance to the long narrow fjord, about reports of enemy activity and was told there were some six German warships up the fjord. Attacking at speed at daybreak, he surprised and sank two of the destroyers, while damaging four others, but as he returned to try and finish off these, the other four emerged from a side-fjord where they'd berthed for the night, and opened fire with 5-inch guns. A shell hit his ship, the 'Hardy's, bridge killing him and everyone else there, except the Paymaster-Lieutenant who then beached the stricken ship; another was sunk and the three survivors sailed for the sea.

The reports brought a powerful naval task force three days later: the battleship 'Warspite' leading a flotilla of nine destroyers and the remaining German ships were sunk. An Allied landing followed soon afterwards, the German contingent withdrew into the surrounding mountains, but by the middle of May it was not only obvious that the position of this Anglo-French outpost, on the way to the Arctic, was going to be untenable, but the Wehrmacht's troops and tanks were now actually pouring into France itself. Between the 4th and 8th of June the force was evacuated and on the 9th the Norwegian Government had no option but to surrender; their Royal Family withdrawing to Britain, where they resided in Scotland with the prominent Salvesen family. As if to underline the changed circumstances in the Scandinavian theatre, the previous day the battle-cruiser 'Scharnhorst', which some weeks earlier had fought an inconclusive engagement with the 'Renown', sank the aircraft carrier 'Glorious', carrying a deckful of invaluable land fighter planes home.

JOHN SWIRE & SONS LIMITED

THE EVACUATION

The first major upheaval of the war actually took place before the state of hostilities existed, when the Government began to implement the elaborate plans which had been in the making throughout the late thirties to evacuate children, and some mothers, including pregnant women, from what were considered the urban danger areas to the comparative safety of the countryside. The thinking had been dictated mainly by the threat of aerial bombing – like the artist's impression of whole cities reduced to a pile of rubble, through which the now liberated carnivors of the erstwhile zoological garden roamed, searching for bodies to eat; and in fact the Spanish Civil War had provided some graphic examples of air raid carnage. It was also in deference to the anticipated house to house fighting after any invasion.

In the event as, not waiting for raids or invasion, the plan was set in motion it soon become clear that it was hardly a uniform national process and some of it beggared logic. Despite the significance of all ports to an island dependent on shipments of food and raw materials (not to mention the *slight* strategic appeal of one of the Royal Navy's most famous bases!) Plymouth, Swansea and Bristol were totally excluded from the scheme (the initial anguish of their inhabitants turning to justified smug relief as it ran its course). And the supposed sanctuary was to be quite discriminatory – in London, plans were to involve less than half of the capital's schoolchildren, the average city 'designated' was about 25 per cent and some, such as Sheffield, would be leaving 85 per cent to their fate. This was really quite understandable: Walter Elliot, whose Ministry of Health was responsible for the Evacuation, rather despairingly described it as bigger then Moses' exodus and involving more organisation than ten Expeditionary Force Armies. The plans called for the relocation of more than 3,500,000 individuals – the actual number was less then 1,500,000, the final breakdown being 827,000 schoolchildren, 524,000 of pre-school age, 12,000 expectant mothers and, with inevitable bureaucracy, 103,000 teachers and 'helpers'.

The Evacuation provided a Press, hungry for war-pathos and human stories, in the face of military non-events at the time, with excellent material; giving the whole exercise an importance and success that was far removed from the facts, which probably accounted for even the numbers that did participate. The newspapers were full of images of small children, labels with the names around their necks, gas mask in a cardboard box, clutching a few belongings in a bag and some personal soft toy – posed pictures with smiles and waves and clearly more factual ones of apprehension and bewilderment; one of the favourites depicting them entering the railway station as troops passed them marching out.

The labels were necessary, too. The waiting trains had to be filled as quickly as possible before taking off to deposit their small passengers wherever their destination happened to be. Some reception centres were inundated with far more than they could cope with; others didn't receive a fraction of what they'd prepared for. At these centres, in many cases sadly, prospective foster parents vied with one another, as though at some sort of auction, for the most appealing and best turned-out children, unreasonably oblivious to the fact that they'd mostly arrived tired, dishevelled and nervous after their first long journey ever.

Much has been said of the mutual incompatibility of these small refugees from the poorer urban areas and their well-to-do country hosts; but it is a fact that many also happily adapted to their new circumstances, learnt much and there was sadness on both sides when the relationships all too often ended. A Punch cartoon portrayed a little girl cheerfully informing her visiting mother. "This is spring, Mummy – they have it here every year." Nevertheless, the most lasting impact of the Evacuation was to underline the social problems and differences that had existed in some quarters of pre-war Britain and undoubtedly the widespread stories had a profound effect on social thinking and policy, as was evidenced by the Beveridge Report, which was published in December 1942, as the country began slowly to plan for a victorious peace.

Meanwhile, a trickle of returning refugees, prompted by homesickness, parental concern – and at that time the failure of the air raid danger to materialise, was under way. With typical official stubbornness, attempts were made to stop this expression of freewill: a poster campaign, including a spectral Hitler urging mothers to bring their children back to town was launched; but with or without the Fuhrer's exhortations, by the spring of 1940 three out of four evacuees had returned home, another scheme launched by the Government failed completely and soon afterwards virtually all families were reunited – blitz or no blitz.

WINSTON CHURCHILL BECOMES PRIME MINISTER

The Norwegian campaign which ended with the Anglo-French withdrawal on 4th June 1940, had signally failed to achieve its dual purpose – to support that country in the face of German aggression, and to stop the supply of iron ore to their war effort from Narvik. It did however have a very positive consequence in ending the 'phoney war' for Britain. And the Norway debate, earlier on 7-8th May, saw the beginning of the end of Neville Chamberlain's premiership (it was during this that a Conservative MP quoted Cromwell at him: "Depart, I say, and let us have done. In the name of God, go".) Forty-one of them voted with the Opposition and sixty abstained – though that still left his Government with a majority of 81. The real fact of the matter was that the mood both at Westminster and in the country was not so much an anti-Chamberlain one, but an instinctive British response to a national emergency by closing the ranks of the Island Race in a Coalition Government. There Chamberlain's difficulty lay. When he asked Clement Attlee and his Labour Executive, meeting at the time in Bournemouth, whether they would join his Government, they declined, and then with what some may regard as typical indecisiveness, qualified this by saying they would serve under 'another Prime Minister'. Chamberlain had to make way, and on the face of it to most Conservatives, Lord Halifax was the obvious successor, on the assumption that the Party would be universally behind him as it entered the coalition arrangement. But next Winston Churchill, who had a growing following, in the light of his persistent and eloquent anti-Nazi stand in the immediate prewar years, and whose warnings had come to pass, refused to serve under Halifax – so he became virtually the only all-round acceptable choice.

Both Chamberlain and Halifax were dubbed to a greater or lesser extent 'appeasers', but the fact is that not only were they far from alone in this supposed role, in all kinds of places, high and low, but this mind-set must be seen in terms of what, predictably, did transpire. In the light of the effects of the First World War, not only in the appalling human suffering, but also the whole fabric of society as it had been known, the effects of another, and obviously technically more devastating world conflict on Britain, the Empire and Western Europe (even then heavily in competition with an ever mightier United States).

The behaviour, and stated principles of the Fascist regimes were manifestly abhorrent and unacceptable, just as those of the Russian Bolsheviks had been and indeed were continuing to be under Stalin – but to try and address these problems first by diplomacy before trying 'other means' was hardly to be deplored.

History would have been different had these efforts succeeded. Instead, there was a war – a war that some estimates put at 55 million dead worldwide. But history is made of facts, not conjecture – and one of those facts was the remarkable good fortune of Britain to find the man for the hour in Winston Churchill, who became Prime Minister on the 10th of May, with his magnificent leadership and his persuasion of the Americans to abandon neutrality. Without him history could well have been different again.

'The Call Up': 27 Section men register for duty in H.M. Forces, 25 May 1940.

THE DUNKIRK WITHDRAWAL FROM THE BEACHES

On 30th May 1940, news of one of the most amazing military operations of all time was made known to the world. Many British, French and Belgian troops had reached the tiny French Channel port of Dunkirk and were already being evacuated from the beaches by a flotilla of 887 craft, both naval and civilian of every size and shape. From 30th May until 3rd June, over 336,000 men in all reached safety. In the painting, troops can be seen on the sands, wading out waist-deep to meet the little boats, that will convey them to the rescuing ships, and drawn up on the beach awaiting the strange navy, gathering to take them to safety. The fires of furiously burning petrol tanks in the town are creating a huge pall of smoke in the background and during the entire time of their long wait to be rescued the men on the beaches were subjected to almost continuous bombing and machine-gun attacks from German planes. Casualties might have been considerably more serious were it not for the British fighters and anti-aircraft batteries which engaged the raiders on the outskirts of Dunkirk.

Waiting their turn to find places in the rescue vessels, the troops at Dunkirk scattered over the neighbouring sand dunes, taking such rough cover as they could find and went down to the beach in batteries as boats became available. Chains of men, neck-deep in water and many still with their rifles and equipment, waded out from the shore to scramble up the sides of the rescue ships to be hailed by such ironic cries from those already aboard as "Keep your socks dry!".

Many of the little boats used in the Dunkirk operation were manned by amateur crews and came from the Thames and coast towns of Southern and South East England. A Thames boat firm acted as a clearing house, collecting small craft of all kinds, especially motor boats and their crews from London's River. The RNVR played an important role in these vital operations. Many of the small craft were damaged or sunk, but most returned to await the resumption of their calmer life as pleasure boats.

Handing over the Ration Book for butter in a London store – Fortnum & Mason.

FAIR SHARES FOR ALL – RATIONING

It was only a matter of weeks before the war served notice that, for most people far from being a matter that concerned someone else somewhere else, it intended to intrude into every household, great and small. The 29th of September was designated 'National Registration Day' when every householder was responsible for filling-in a form that had been sent to them with the personal details of everyone resident there. The next day the forms were collected, and an identity card, a piece of light blue folded cardboard was issued by an official with the number, name and address of the holder, whose only authorised contribution was his/her signature – anything else could result in 'a fine or imprisonment or both' and which made provision for every change of address. 'Food Officers' used the information from the forms, and each person's National Registration Number to supply them, by post with a personalised Ration Book, a small beige booklet with page after page of coupons printed with the day of the week in which they were to be used, to be clipped off by a shopkeeper and retained for possible inspection by a Ministry of Food Inspector, who ensured that it tallied with food supplied to the shop – everyone was required to register their Ration Book with their own grocer and butcher who would then apply for the total quantity of food involved from the Ministry.

The system began in November 1939 when the population were warned to register with a retailer as butter and bacon were shortly to be rationed; sugar following suit soon afterwards. Meanwhile, down on the farm, plans had been made that it was hoped would double the yield from the land, though a prolonged severe frost retarded this that winter by holding up ploughing.

Rationing actually commenced on 8th January 1940 and on that day weekly allowances per person were fixed at: 4oz of butter, 4oz of bacon or ham and 12oz of sugar. There were three types of Books in operation: the General Book (RB1) for all adults, children becoming grown-up after their sixth birthday; the Childrens' Book (RB2) for those below that age (extra 'growth foods' such as milk and orange juice were to be allowed when rationing reached these items) and Special Category books such as Seaman's and Travellers, for lorry drivers, etc.

In fact, apart from the restricted categories of foodstuffs shoppers were at first able to enjoy plenty of choice in imported lines. At the outbreak of war, the U-Boat campaign took some months to build up into anything like a stranglehold and the Ministry of Food were able to import many millions of pounds worth from all corners of the globe.

On 11th March meat went on rationing, the obvious difficulties being resolved by basing the allowance not on weight but by price: the housewife found what she could get depended on the ruling price of each cut, and obviously more of the lower end of the scale could be obtained than of prime steak for a given number of coupons. The weekly allowance for an adult was 1s 10d (now about 9p), a child under six 11d (4½p.) Restaurants were allowed 1d (½p) per couvert and coalminers' canteens a generous 2d (1p) per meal. For many the grim writing on the wall was all to obvious when on the 7th July tea was restricted to 2oz per week, followed by margarine and cooking fats also at 2oz on the 22nd.

In retrospect, Britain was now entering its worst food crisis of the war which was from July 1940 to June 1941 with the steeply mounting loss of food ships as they approached the home ports and the land production's ultimate performance at that time still thwarted by teething troubles of organisation and undertrained civilian staff. The nadir was reached in the spring of 1941 when the average diet reached an alarmingly low ebb with meat allowances drastically reduced and a whole range of foods including milk and fish in very short supply, while jam was a luxury and even the onion was so scarce that many a stew of what there was suffered fatally. Cheese was in such short supply that it fell to only 1oz per week, a quantity that was too small to cut practically for most varieties, so it had to be done by the month.

Of the staple necessities, bread – and to many more importantly beer – escaped the system but even they were frequently in short supply.

Rationing had been introduced in Germany a full year before the actual outbreak of war (which must have made the thoughtful wonder, especially as the British Government studied it to see if any lessons could be learnt) and as, even in pre-war years, the Third Reich cultivated the people with a powerful propaganda machine, it was widely and readily accepted as a national duty. In Britain it was reluctantly accepted as inevitable (after it happened, prior to that nobody would have seen it as their duty nor indeed believed it would happen). At the end of the day, despite some degree of maladministration and black marketeering it was seen to have been a fair system and it had also encouraged a certain cheerful self-reliance and resourcefulness in many people.

The extensive queueing, especially in all weathers, took longer to come to terms with – but even that became a way of life: arriving in a town where he was a stranger, a man noticed a queue of unusual length and immediately concluded that a bonus supply of 'something' had been released and joined the end. After a while he asked the woman in front what 'it' was; "Tales of Hofmann" she replied. "It's amazing what we'll eat nowadays", he mused.

THE HOME GUARD

On the 14 May 1940, as the German Army crossed the Meuse River and it was clear that it would soon pass through Flanders into France itself the 'phoney war' became a little less so for many, who found themselves far more involved, after a broadcast appeal by Churchill's new War Secretary, Anthony Eden:

"Since the war began the Government has received enquiries from men of all ages, from all over the Kingdom, who are not in the Armed Services for one reason or another, as to what part they can play. Well, here is your opportunity. We want large numbers of men, who are British Subjects, between the ages of 17 and 65, to come forward and offer their services in a new force to be called 'Local Defence Volunteers'".

It was to be triumphantly reported that even before the broadcast finished volunteers had arrived at their local police stations, within 24 hours 250,000 had enrolled and by the end of the following month, June, the total was over 1⅓ million. On the 14th of July, Winston Churchill, with his genius for phraseology, referred to the new citizens' army as the 'Home Guard' and the name stuck. Eden had promised the volunteers "you will receive a uniform and be armed': fortunately for him without specifying further – for a considerable time the only uniform was an 'HG' armband and the weapons could have rendered a valuable service in cataloguing man's inhumanity to man over the centuries – pikestaffs, to assegai souvenirs from the Zulu wars through to modern devastation such a cache of rusty Lee Enfields donated by the props room of the Theatre Royal, Drury Lane, who couldn't envisage many imminent performances of 'All quiet on the Western Front'. And the countryman's shotgun was given a ringing endorsement by no less than the C-in-C Home Forces himself with the comforting and useful reassurance that "with solid ammunition – it could kill a leopard at 300 yards."

The duties of the Home Guard, which in its initial years was more like 'Grandad's Army' because of the high average age of its intake, was to mount patrols, the first such being achieved by the 'Worthing Battalion of the Sussex Home Guard' on 15th May.

Apart from the patrols guarding their localities, including critical areas for parachute invasion, such as the local golfcourse, ideal for glider landings, 'observation corps' duties were also a fundamental activity; if the terrain included it, the post might be on top of the local hill, up which men of advancing years would slog, to spend hours in whatever shelter, if any, could be provided looking for anything 'suspicious' in the landscape or sky. Depending on the locality, and type of community, the pre-occupation with paratroops, whom it was believed would spearhead any invasion, was sometimes paranoid. It was certain they would arrive in disguise – dressed as nuns was the most common assumption and everyone was advised to study their footwear (it's not recorded what further investigation was followed with any who had larger than average feet). In fact in many places, with the prevailing psychosis about fifth columnists, saboteurs and 'despondency-spreaders', strangers were well advised to watch their step – and tongue. To drive at night was also to court suspicious attention in rural areas. As a doctor recalled: "Coming round a bend, I nearly ran down an uncouth lout wielding some historical firearm. It looked highly dangerous, both to him and myself, and I refused to speak to him till he put it down on the grass verge. After that, he perused my papers, using my sidelights though it was obvious he was quite illiterate."

There were also the 'post-invasion' exercises. The village high street would be blocked with anything from old beds and mattresses to felled saplings and the anti-tank brigade would secrete themselves behind a hedge. When the panzer column obligingly halted at the obstruction, the lead tank (which bore a remarkable resemblance to an old Riley) was pelted with 'Molotov cocktails' (understudied by bags of chalk and soot) after it had indeed been reduced to a very sorry sight, the second, which had been waiting patiently for attention was dispatched by the furious attack of a stirrup-pump – standing-in for a flame-thrower.

In the summer of 1943 there were 1100 Home Guard Battalions, totalling 1.75 million men; since 1942 the preponderant new recruits were teenagers, including organisations such as the Eton College Cadet Corps who were co-opted into it, and the average age dropped to under thirty; 'Dad's Army' was now only seven per cent. And by 1943 the uniform appearance and weaponry were much closer to the Regular Army's infantry and the organisation considerably better: it is ironic that the Home Guard only achieved any real effectiveness after the danger of any invasion had passed. This People's Army in what, with the Blitz and home privations, was very much a People's War, had however achieved a very useful psychological purpose in the darkest days after Dunkirk till El Alamein, the arrival of the Americans, the Russian Front and the retaliation of RAF and US. Air Force bombing had changed the whole atmosphere. It also relieved the Regular Army of many guard duties on the Home Front, enabling the much needed retraining to be far more rapidly undertaken; and it even provided some sort of induction into Service life for sixteen and seventeen year olds awaiting their call-up.

The Home Guard was stood down at the end of November 1944. It was marked by a spectacular showbusiness tribute concert with Vera Lynn and many others at the Royal Albert Hall, organised by the *Daily Mail*.

HURRICANES ENGAGE STUKAS AND MESSERSCHMITTS OVER DOVER

In the opening phases of the Battle of Britain, the Germans attacked the British coastal convoys, ports, radar stations, and advanced airfields, and among the aircraft used was the vaunted Junkers 87 dive bomber (in the German Air Force all dive bombers, regardless of manufacture, were known as "Stukas", but to the British the name has become linked witht he JU 87). This aircraft had enjoyed great success during the Polish and French campaigns, but against a well organised defence and opposition, such as that provided by RAF Fighter Command, they lost heavily. After a disastrous series of defeats the JU 87 was largely withdrawn from the Battle after 18 August 1940 – a tactical victory to the RAF of some importance.

The Hurricane in the foreground is from No. 32 Squadron, which, in the early stages of the Battle, was based at Biggin Hill, one of the RAF's most famous Battle of Britain airfields. The squadron was hotly engaged in a number of fiercely disputed engagements in the early stages of the Battle and claimed a number of victories.

The squadron, during this time, often used Hawkinge, near Folkestone, as an advanced base, and after suffering some losses in pilots and aircraft was sent, in August 1940, to Acklington to rest and train new pilots.

Somewhat overshadowed in the popular mind by the Spitfire, the Hurricane was a robust aircraft and was credited with the destruction of about four-fifths of the total of enemy aircraft destroyed in the Battle. The Hurricane equipped the majority of Fighter Command squadrons at this period.

The Messerschmitt 109E diving away smoking in the left centre of the painting is typical of the fighter aircraft arrayed against the RAF during the Battle. An aircraft bearing the "Red 14" markings of the second staffel of Jagdgeschwader 52 (2/JG52) was forced to land near Lewes, Sussex, on 12 August 1942, and the wounded pilot was captured.

CHARLES CUNDALL: I.W.M.

FIGHTER CONTROL ROOM AT UXBRIDGE

One of the most closely guarded pre-war secrets of the RAF was the development and use of Radar (then known as RDF or Radio Direction Finding). Apart from the British development of radar and the solution of its many technical problems, the advantage which this technological achievement conferred could only be realised if the problems surrounding its tactical use could also be solved.

Previously envisaged as a means of locating incoming enemy bombers at a far enough distance to enable adequate warning to be given, the radar (RDF) stations had to be linked to a control and reporting system so that incoming information from the radar stations (over sea plots) and the Observer Corps (over land plots) could be evaluated and instructions to defending fighters issued.

There were several Fighter Groups, each responsible for an area of Great Britain in Fighter Command. This painting shows the operations room at Uxbridge, the HQ of No. 11 Group which covered the South-East of England.

Each of the WAAF fighter plotters surrounding the map is in contact with a radar station, and as information reaches her she places the necessary counters with the information on to the map. Seated above them, in a glazed balcony, thus sound-proofed, are the various staff officers and controllers who will order fighter squadrons to take off as required. Changes of course (vectors) can be given after the take off as the tactical situation requires, using the latest information displayed on the map. In this way the defending fighters being directed to the attack are using information which was often only a few minutes old. Similarly, the Group Commander can direct his squadrons in battle in a manner only dreamed of a few years before.

On the wall opposite the controllers are "tote boards" which display information about each squadron – e.g. "stand-by", "released", "takeoff", etc.

This means of controlling fighters has become almost worldwide, and any air defence system must use a similar system today.

Fighter Command (Stanmore), November 1940
– No. 9 Group, Preston
– No. 10 Group, Box
– No. 11 Group, Uxbridge
– No. 12 Group, Watnall
– No. 13 Group, Newcastle
– No. 14 Group, Inverness

INDUSTRIA ENGINEERING PRODUCTS LTD

FRANK WOOTTON

BATTLE OF BRITAIN OVER THE THAMES VALLEY

After the fall of France in June 1940, and the Italian declaration of war on Britain and its allies on the 10th of that month, Adolf Hitler, who was secretly working on plans to attack his then ally, Russia, realised that he would first either have to negotiate Britain out of the war – or invade. The attempts, with peace feelers through Vatican channels, having failed, the alternative, code-named Operation Seelöwe (Sealion), was then put into effect. The German Army and Navy High Commands correctly advised the Fuhrer that no invasion would be possible unless air superiority over the Channel and South East England was a definite fact – Hermann Goering incorrectly advised that his Luftwaffe would effectively eliminate the RAF from south of a line drawn from Chelmsford to Gloucester, in just four days – the Battle of Britain was their attempt to do so.

At the beginning of August attacks were stepped up on convoys to lure the RAF into fighting over the Channel, where a pilot shot down would probably be lost, but the Commander-in-Chief of Fighter Command, Air Marshal Sir Hugh Dowding and his officer for the South East, Air Vice Marshal Park, refused to be drawn (just as Dowding had opposed the deployment of ten squadrons in France, in May) and so the Battle proper began on 12 August with raids on five coastal radar stations and various aerodromes in Kent and the approaches to London. The following day eleven bases were bombed and on 15 August four massive waves of planes, including bombers from Norway attacking the North East, were deployed at the same targets. The salient facts of the contest were now beginning to emerge. The types of aircraft were about balanced: the RAF's Spitfires, and more numerous Hurricanes, were of similar performance to the Messerschmitt 109s, at 300 mph, and though they lacked comparable firepower, with eight 303 machine-guns as opposed to the latter's cannon, they could turn more tightly, with obvious advantages in the dog-fights. A decisive advantage for the defenders was the range limitation of all fighters: though the Luftwaffe operated from its new bases in north east France, their endurance over England was very limited – only ten minutes over London. This was enhanced by the very effective use of early warning from the, constantly repaired, radar stations – use that was the outstanding contribution of the Control centres, particularly Uxbridge, whereby Fighter Command's tactics could be co-ordinated with up-to-the-minute information that eliminated much waste of time, fuel and ammunition.

The manpower on both sides was highly trained and technically competent,

but here a psychological difference intervened in the real event of war. The Royal Air Force Volunteer Reserve was a major constituent in the Service and these university educated practical young men brought a contribution to the 'regular' tactics, of fresh thinking and highly individual action, to an activity that was basically one man's efforts in his own cockpit. And there was the motivation: whatever that of Goering's professionals, flying to attack yet another country, it couldn't be matched by that of men who saw their own country really threatened by invasion for the first time in 900 years – and there was a large contingent of Czechs and Poles with every incentive, too.

A pattern of losses soon emerged; typical was 15 August with 34 RAF planes to 76 of the enemy – during the whole Battle the figures wee 650 to 1100, respectively. Nevertheless, Goering persisted, believing the RAF's rate of attrition far worse than it was – and at last it began to pay off, as sheer exhaustion, more of pilots than aircraft, took its inevitable toll, in a summer of perfect flying weather. The 31st of August was the worst single day, and the first week of September suggested what some began to believe was the beginning of the end for Fighter Command: though 225 German planes had been shot down, that was now costing 185 British. But it was in fact the beginning of something else. On the night of 25 August the RAF bombed Berlin; if it was an *agence provocateur* strategy it, predictably, worked. On 7 September all day was one of unnerving quiet – till in the late afternoon over 400 bombers, accompanied by 600 fighters, blackened the skies – only to overfly their battered targets, en route to London's East End. 'The miracle' as Dowding was to describe it, was caused by Hitler's direct intervention with orders for a retaliation raid. And the same targets were preferred in the following days. The battle had hung by a thread, however this crucial breathing space gave Fighter Command the opportunity to regroup, re-equip and rest pilots. By 15 September, now Battle of Britain Day, the initiative had been wrested from the Luftwaffe, on that day two massive wings of bombers, with heavy fighter protection, were attacked and dispersed by a revitalised defence. Whatever Goering continued to say, Hitler drew his own conclusions – two days later the invasion plans were indefinitely postponed.

As Churchill said 'Never was so much owed by so many to so few' – the war had not been won, but it had been saved, a German invasion would unquestionably have been the end of it, in only 1940, just twelve months after it had begun.

The gallant Jervis Bay sacrifices herself for her convoy.

The San Demetrio berths in the Clyde, her crew on deck

HOLMAN, FENWICK & WILLAN

THE SAVING OF THE 'SAN DEMETRIO'

In September 1940 the 'San Demetrio', a modern oil tanker owned by the Eagle Oil and Shipping Company which merged with Shell Tankers in 1960, left Aruba laden with 11,200 tons of badly needed petroleum and proceeded to Halifax, Nova Scotia, where she joined a UK-bound convoy of 38 ships, which sailed on the 26th October escorted by the armed merchant cruiser 'Jervis Bay'.

In the late afternoon of 5th November, in position of long. 32 W and lat. 52 30 N, she sighted a vessel approaching on her port beam in the gloom. Soon afterwards the 'Jervis Bay' was seen to turn to port, signalling as she did so that she was engaging the German pocket-battleship 'Admiral Scheer' and ordering the convoy to scatter at best speed. Heavily outgunned, the 'Jervis Bay' closed with the enemy and fought to the finish and this action ultimately gave 32 ships of the convoy time to escape; her Commander Captain Fogarty Fegen RN being awarded a posthumous Victoria Cross. Dropping smoke floats, the 'San Demetrio' made off; but out of the darkness a salvo that straddled her was followed by a third that caused extensive damage, including a large hole on the port bow just above the waterline, and the ship was abandoned in three lifeboats, which, as they fell away astern, saw her burst into flames.

Losing touch with the others (who were subsequently rescued) Second Officer Arthur Hawkins navigated No. 1 boat through mountainous seas for two days before sighting a ship – which turned out to be the blazing 'San Demetrio'. Hoisting a sail he overtook her and at first light the sixteen men unanimously agreed to reboard their ship. With great difficulty the only quarter unaffected by fire, her stern, was climbed by a trailing lifeboat fall. The 'San Demetrio' was in critical condition: a fierce fire raged aft of where the bridge had been – that had been completely carried away with all the navigation aids, charts and the steering gear itself; the decks glowed hot in places and ominously, each time she rolled great spurts of petrol shot high into the air where the tanktops had been pierced by shell splinters, and then swilled round the hot decks. Most of the accommodation and all the food stores had been destroyed: all that remained were some loaves of bread, tinned butter, tea and condensed milk and some potatoes (which couldn't be cooked as all-pervading petrol fumes precluded lighting the stove) which happened to be in the galley aft when the attack started. There was already eight feet of water in the forepeak and more entered through the hole in the bow with every roll – and to add to all this the weather was deteriorating.

On the positive side, though the engineroom was flooded to the floorplates, the main engines were undamaged and though the aft steering wheel had been reduced to only two spokes the rudder still responded to that manual gear. Six hours saw sufficient steam pressure to man the firehoses and after all hands had spent an entire night tackling them, all fires had been extinguished; and with the danger of fanning them gone, the main engines were started and at 2.35 pm on 8th November a pocketbook log recorded 'San Demetrio' underway again. Although the normal engineroom complement of 14 hands was now replaced by only four, and one of those, John Boyle died after three days from internal injuries received on boarding the lifeboat and was buried at sea next daybreak,

a speed of nine knots was maintained night and day. There were also only four capable of alternating at the helm and steering was extremely difficult as a series of NW gales kept setting her to southward; in addition being well-down by the head made the ship very 'tender', as large quantities of water entered the hole in the bow. They tried to trim the vessel by draining the forward tanks, but the pumps wouldn't respond; however they did manage to drain No.s 9 p and c tanks into a centre tank, which kept the hole further above the waves. Asked later how he had navigated without chart or sextant, Hawkins explained that he'd used the Pole Star to establish an easterly heading, checking whenever the sky permitted by sun and moon and he always "knew Ireland was there". All the crew behaved "magnificently" – and tirelessly, working any hours necessary in a darkened ship (even an oil-lamp could not be risked with the fumes) in freezing cold in a North Atlantic winter, living on the most meagre rations of only cold food. With the lifeboat water-logged and carried away they were also only too well aware that if they ran into any further trouble, such as being torpedoed, they now possessed no means of escape.

It was indeed a great team effort, but subsequently the crew singled out one man for special praise. Oswald Preston had signed on in Halifax as a Nova Scotian, but once aboard it was discovered that he was an American whose only interest was to get to Britain and join one of the fighting forces. He showed a "marked disinclination for any sort of work" – till the raider struck. He'd kept up the spirits of all in the lifeboat by his humorous and optimistic attitude, he was the first to manage to reboard the ship and he returned over the said in a vain effort to save the lifeboat; he "did the work of two men" throughout and was "simply magnificent". When the ship did reach port her Red Ensign, which had flown throughout, was presented by the men to their American shipmate. On 13th November, after a voyage of 700 miles under these conditions, a landfall was made. There was no means of communicating with the shore in the absence of flags and wireless, nor could the anchor be dropped as the steam winches to heave it up had been destroyed, so 'San Demetrio' cruised what proved to be Blacksod Bay all night. Fortunately someone alerted the Admiralty and in the morning a destroyer, 'Arrow', arrived; accompanied by her, Hawkins and his crew insisted on sailing their brave ship into the Clyde where she arrived at 9.30 pm on the 16th of November, with 10,000 tons of her precious cargo intact.

The tanker's crew were justifiably civically feted and her owners suggested that the men should put in a claim for salvage services rendered, offering to underwrite their legal costs, whatever the outcome, when it was heard in the Admiralty Division. This took place on the 16th and 17th January 1941, the prominent firm of experts in Maritime Law, Holman, Fenwick & Willan appearing in the case, which duly awarded a substantial sum which was divided amongst the men (and the representative of John Boyle who'd died).

Sadly, the eventful life of "San Demetrio" ended when the submarine U404 torpedoed her 80 miles east of Chesapeake Bay, on the 17th of March 1942.

THE POWER FOR VICTORY

FRANK WOOTTON

Rolls-Royce Merlin/Griffon engines on the production line, Derby 1944.

TERENCE CUNEO

ROLLS-ROYCE plc

Above: One of the classic photographs of the war – a German He III bomber drones over London's Isle of Dogs in September 1940.

Left: A pall of smoke hangs over the London docks on the first day of the Blitz, 7 September 1940.

HAMBROS PLC

25

picture: HULTON DEUTSCH

BLITZ DOESN'T STOP MILKMAN

Top: *During the War Period many Salesman were called up for active service. However the remainder, together with sales women, did a yeoman job in making certain that their customers received their daily pinta, despite adverse conditions*

Left: *Many shops were destroyed through enemy action. However, this did not stop trade being carried out by Dairy Retailers who cleared away the debris and reopened as soon as possible, albeit without glass in their windows and ceilings above their heads. Here London Transport bus, which has nosedived into a crater, produced by a direct hit on Balham Tube Station, on 14 October 1940. Of 6,000 people sheltering in the station, 64 drowned in floodwater from shattered waterpipes.*

UNIGATE PLC

ROBERT TAYLOR, The Fleet Air Arm Museum

FLEET AIR ARM ATTACK ON TARANTO

On the night of 11/12 November 1940, a brilliantly planned and executed attack was made by 21 Swordfish aircraft, from the aircraft carriers HMS EAGLE and HMS ILLUSTRIOUS, on capital ships of the Italian fleet, at anchor in Taranto harbour.

Originally, the attack was planned for Trafalgar Day – 21 October – but had to be postponed due to an accidental hangar fire on board ILLUSTRIOUS. Then the EAGLE was found to have her aircraft fuel supply contaminated by seawater and was withdrawn at the last minute. Five of her aircraft from 813 and 824 Squadrons transferred to ILLUSTRIOUS to join the attack with the aircraft of 815 and 819 Squadrons already embarked on ILLUSTRIOUS. Eventually, HMS ILLUSTRIOUS, commanded by her Captain Dennis Boyd RN and with Rear Admiral Lyster, the originator of the plan, embarked set sail with the Mediterranean Fleet from Alexandria.

Last minute reconnaissance photographs showed not only the disposition of the Italian Fleet, but also the formidable enemy defences, including a balloon barrage and anti-torpedo nets around the larger ships.

At 1800, when the Mediterranean Fleet was to the west of the Island of Zante, HMS ILLUSTRIOUS was detached with an escort of cruisers and destroyers to the flying-off point. The 21 Swordfish aircraft took off in two waves, an hour apart. The first wave was airborne at 2057 at a position some 170 miles distance from Taranto. The attack was pressed home with bombs and torpedoes against fierce defensive anti-aircraft fire from the Italian ships and shore batteries. From beginning to end, the first torpedo strike lasted only five minutes. After it, the 35,000 ton battleship LITTORIO was badly damaged and the 23,000 ton CAVOUR was sinking. The bombing attack took longer and after the final wave of aircraft completed their assault, they left two battleships (LITTORIO and CAVOUR) partly under water, another battleship (*Caio Duilo*) severely damaged, two cruisers badly listing to starboard and two fleet auxiliaries with their sterns under water. Subsidiary attacks also succeeded in setting fire to oil storage tanks and wrecking the sea-plane base. Only two British aircraft were lost in the entire action.

Admiral Cunningham, Commander in Chief Mediterranean Fleet, wrote of the attack – "Taranto and the night of 11/12 November 1940, should be remembered forever as having shown, once and for all, that in the Fleet Air Arm, the Navy has its most devastating weapon. In a total flying time of about six and a half hours – carrier to carrier – twenty aircraft had inflicted more damage upon the Italian Fleet than was inflicted upon the German High Seas Fleet in daylight action at the Battle of Jutland."

The benefits of Taranto were seen quite quickly and its result decisively altered the balance of naval power in the Mediterranean.

THE RANK ORGANISATION PLC

BRISTOL BREWERY BOMBED – BUT TAKE COURAGE

Arthur Hadley, head brewer of Georges' Bristol Brewery, ruefully surveys a bomb hole in the brewery roof on the morning of 25 November 1940, after a particularly heavy raid on Bristol the night before.

Left: *London Can Take It. A soldier makes his point with a stained glass panel retrieved from a bomb-damaged pub after the raid of 29 December, 1940.*

COURAGE CHARITABLE TRUST

John Hamilton, I.W.M.

MINESWEEPING TRAWLERS UNDER ATTACK

During the Second World War the fishermen of the British Isles were once again called upon to serve their country. In September 1939, the Admiralty began to requisition trawlers, for deployment as minesweepers, convoy escorts, and anti-submarine vessels. Manned by R.N.R. fishermen they became part of the Royal Navy Patrol Service. The painting above illustrates Junkers 87 divebombers, which can be seen attacking minesweeping trawlers in the Thames estuary, during October 1940. Minesweepers were frequently subject to air attacks, especially in the waters off the south east of England, and along the east coast, as air cover could not always be provided. At the beginning of the war, both Britain and Germany laid prodigious quantities of mines, during the first four months of hostilities 79 Allied merchant ships were sunk by enemy mines in home waters. The trawlers served with great distinction. The larger vessels worked in convoys across the stormy Atlantic Ocean, the Artic run to Murmansk, and in the tropical heat to South Aftrica.

H.M.T Marette, 135ft. 350 ton trawler, built for J. Marr & Son Ltd in 1929. Pennant No FY 665.

'Celerity' ML 241. One of the vessels owned by St Monan's fisherman.

ASSOCIATED FISHERIES plc   J. MARR LIMITED   THE SCOTTISH FISHERIES MUSEUM TRUST LTD

This emergency shop was one of two Sainsbury's delivery vans converted to serve customers when bombing incidents made it impossible to trade normally.

THE EMERGENCY SHOP

As a company that had long specialised in the retailing of meat, dairy produce and bacon, and whose trading heartland was in London and the South-East, Sainsbury's had to strive to maintain standards of quality and service during the food shortages and bombing raids of wartime. Advertisements were placed in national newspapers to explain the food controls. In 1940, the company introduced its own 'Fair Shares' scheme using 'points' to ensure that goods which were in short supply but not government rationed, such as sausages and meat pies, were distributed equally. Despite that scheme, many customers were frustrated by the long queues that formed for unrationed items, and to ease the situation, Sainsbury's developed a system known as 'call-backs', to enable customers to leave a shopping list at the store and call back later to collect their purchases. This was particularly useful for working people with little time to shop, and in some areas Sainsbury's shops remained open late one evening a week to enable workers to collect their orders.

Rationing was by no means the only problem as air raids intensified. At the start of the war, managers were instructed to close their shops as soon as the sirens sounded, and to post a notice on the doorpost stating the location of the nearest ARP shelter. However, many customers preferred to stay on the premises rather than go to the crowded shelters. Whenever possible, benches made of egg stall boards, and trestles were set up in the shop basements for them. If no basement was available, it was suggested that 'quite good cover is to be had beneath the counter or back shelf', which at that time was constructed from solid marble slabs. If a Sainsbury shop was bombed out, or a road closed, trade was continued from improvised shop counters out on the street, or from one of two mobile emergency shops set up at the back of converted delivery vehicles. One customer at Walthamstow remembered the efforts of the elderly manager there to reopen his wrecked shop following a bad night of bombing. The police had brought him from his home at 2.00 in the morning, and the poor old chap had spent his time dusting off the bacon and scraping soot from the margarine.

DON'T SHOOT THE MAN BEHIND THE COUNTER: This advertisement from 1939 urged Sainsbury's customers to have patience with staff during the food shortages.

The dome of St Paul's Cathedral rises majestic and unscathed above the fires raised at the height of the incendiary attack on London on 29 December, 1940.

BLITZ FIRES HIGHLIGHT ST PAUL'S

During the Blitz on London there was only one occasion on which the Luftwaffe threatened to create conditions similar to those which, after Allied raids, were to lead to the terrible firestorms in Hamburg (1943) and Dresden (1945). On Sunday, 29 December 1940, an incendiary raid on the City of London was compounded by a neap-tide, which made it all but impossible for the hoses of the fire brigade to reach down to the river. Shops and offices were locked up and the firewatchers, who were still volunteers, off duty. The two-hour attack, by the relatively small number of 150 aircraft, started some 1500 fires, of which 90 per cent raged virtually unchecked in the City, fanned by a strong westerly wind. One conflagration, which consumed everything between Moorgate, Aldersgate Street, Cannon Street and Old Street, produced the biggest area of war devastation in Great Britain.

On the edge of this sea of fire stood St Paul's Cathedral, its dome rising majestically above the dense clouds of black smoke. St Paul's was hit by at least twenty-eight incendiaries, one of which stuck halfway through the outer shell of the dome. Had it fallen through onto the beams and dry timbers of the inner dome, St Paul's might well have burned down. Miraculously the incendiary suddenly slid off and fell on to the Stone Gallery, where it was quickly extinguished.

That night a Bethnal Green woman had donned her tin hat and ventured into the inferno in the City. 'I went up on the roof with some of the firemen to look at the City. And I've always remembered how I was choked, I think I was crying a little. I could see St Paul's standing there, and the fire all around, and I just said, "Please God, don't let it go!"'

ROCKPOOL

THE GALLANT MERCHANT NAVY

In W.W.2 the Ropner fleet lost 33 ships from enemy action (in W.W.1 losses had numbered 28) U-boat torpedoes accounted for 21 of the sinkings, German surface craft for 5, mines for 5, air attack for 1 and 1 was captured alongside berth in the Norwegian campaign.

Two Ropner ships, Stonepool and Rockpool, were each successful in disabling U-boats that were subsequently sunk by Royal Navy destroyers; both soon after the outbreak of war in October 1939. These actions were responsible (in addition to the sinkings by Ropner ships of 2 U-boats in W.W.1) for the legend of "Ropners Navy".

The following is an excerpt from the "Ropner Story" by Ian Dear published by Hutchinson Benham in 1986.

"Rockpool" in a convoy of ten ships out of Newfoundland and loaded with ore, was battling against a full Atlantic gale. At 0500, well before dawn, her port lifeboat was partly carried away and her master, Captain Harland, signalled the commodore of the convoy for permission to heave to. In the darkness and the severe weather conditions they could not make contact with the commodore but Captain Harland decided to heave to anyway. The lifeboat was retrieved, but at dawn "Rockpool" found herself alone. She failed to find the convoy again and by 19 October had entered the Western Approaches, an area extensively patrolled by U-boats. On returning from his lunch below to the bridge Captain Harland at once saw a U-boat to starboard and as he gave urgent orders for the ship to swing away the submarine opened fire.

Captain Harland later reported to his owners:

I ordered the helm hard a port, called all hands to their stations and sent out a radio. He fired four or five rounds very quickly but did not get a hit. We opened fire and at the third shot he submerged. After about three or four minutes he commenced to rise. As soon as his periscope came above the surface we opened fire. He fired several rounds of shrapnel, the shells bursting just clear of the bows. We got close to him. Through the binoculars you could see the spray from our shells going over his conning tower. He again submerged for a few minutes. The battle went on like this until 1345. He was working out a very good bracket and at any moment I expected to be hit. When we dropped our shells close to him he dived. At 1345 I ordered smoke floats to be thrown over the side. At 1350 the smoke screen was effective and we got away without any damage to the ship or crew. I must in concluding say the morale of the crew was astonishing, there was no panic, every man carried out instantly the orders that were given. At 1600 I put the firemen on double watches and kept them doubled until we passed Lundy Island. This was the only way they could keep a full head of steam.

To this dispassionate account of a battle fought over more than ten miles Captain Harland added a brief postscript. "Since writing the above letter, I have been informed by the Admiralty that we so damaged the submarine that he could not submerge. A destroyer coming in answer to my radio captured the survivors and sank the submarine. I did not see the destroyer". In December 1939 Captain Harland was awarded the OBE. The citation for Captain Harland's decoration read:

A U-boat suddenly appeared on the scene at about one and a half miles distance, and immediately fired a shot which fell about 100 yards short. The second shot was close on the quarter. The Master at once altered helm to bring the U-boat astern and his gun into action. He fired thirteen rounds, which fell so close that the enemy was drenched with spray. The U-boat fired some twenty rounds, and Rockpool was straddled, but not hit. After a stern chase of an hour and a quarter she shook off the enemy by zigzagging behind a screen of smoke floats. The crew showed great coolness under fire, and all who could helped in the action. The master handled his ship in a seamanlike manner and deserves great praise for his coolness and judgment, and for the readiness and efficiency of his ship's company. The U-boat which he was the first to sight, was in due course destroyed by the Royal Navy.

In a similar citation the Rockpool's gunner, ex-Colour Sergeant Thomas

VALLDEMOSA

VALLDEMOSA was a 10,000 tons deadweight tanker, built at Lithgows, Port Glasgow. The only ship, out of six tankers owned by Gow, Harrison & Co. to survive World War II.

The other 5 ships that were lost during enemy action were: VOREDA. Bombed and set on fire 30 January 1940. VENETIA. Torpedoed, sunk by gun fire 18 March 1941. VANCOUVER. Mined and sunk 21 September 1941. VIRGILIA. Torpedoed and sunk 24 November 1941. VIMEIRA. Torpedoed and sunk 11 August 1942.

Harrisons (Clyde) Limited is the successor to the old Glasgow firm, Gow Harrison & Co., the first tanker owners in Scotland. The present Company, incorporated in 1956, has been involved in most aspects of the shipping business, both as owners and managers. Its principal activity today, through its subsidiary, Stirling Shipping Company Limited, is in the owning of a fleet of offshore supply vessels, operating mainly in the North Sea. Harrisons (Clyde) Limited also participates in the joint venture ownership of a diving vessel and a survey vessel, and manages Western Ferries (Clyde) Limited which operates a very successful RO/RO service across the Clyde between Gourock and Dunoon.

WINAMAC

The Winamac was torpedoed and sunk, position undetermined but in the southern half of the North Atlantic, on 31 August 1942. Twenty six lives were lost.

In May 1941 fifty American oil tankers were transferred to Britain:

In March 1942 the abolition of the Civilian 'Basic Ration' of petrol took most people's cars off the road. Commercial petrol was dyed red. In terms of the war effort a bomber required 2,000 gallons of petrol to reach the Rühr. The loss of the Winamac gives one an idea how hard it was to get fuel to this country.

HARRISONS (CLYDE) LIMITED

MOBIL SHIPPING COMPANY LIMITED

ROPNER PLC

ONE OF THE FEW

IN THE HOUR OF PERIL
HOVIS LIMITED
EARNED THE GRATITUDE
OF THE BRITISH NATIONS
SUSTAINING THE VALOUR OF
THE ROYAL AIR FORCE
AND FORTIFYING THE CAUSE
OF FREEDOM
BY THE GIFT OF
SPITFIRE AIRCRAFT
They shall mount up with wings as eagles
*Issued by the Ministry of Aircraft Production
1941*

The Spitfire presented by the Directors of Hovis Limited to the Ministry of Aircraft Production on 20th April 1940. Appropriately christened 'Hominis vis', the latin phrase for 'the strength of man', from which the name 'Hovis' was derived in 1890.

RANK HOVIS LIMITED

KING EDWARD HOUSE • KING EDWARD COURT • WINDSOR • BERKSHIRE • ENGLAND

THE SPITFIRE FUND

Of all the various opportunities for a direct financial contribution to the war effort launched, the Spitfire Fund was the most successful – encouraging companies, groups and even individuals to 'buy' one of the aircraft. A Spitfire was priced at £5,000 and a bomber at £20,000. Sadly, only a few donors opted for the Hurricane, the doughty and robust aircraft that did not have the same glamourous image in the public mind – which could not of course be informed at the time that in its Finest Hour the Royal Air Force fighter squadrons were mostly equipped with Hurricanes, which shot down four-fifths of the enemy aircraft destroyed in the Battle of Britain.

In an imaginative and skilfull exercise, people were involved with a breakdown of the cost of equipment – sixpence for a rivet, fifteen shillings for a blast tube for a machine-gun, £22 for a small bomb, £2,000 for a wing, etc.

By the Spring of 1941 over £13 million had been raised by the Spitfire Fund – on the Home Front, Victory had in fact been secured by the Many for the Few.

London Blitz – May 1941, the end of 23 Queen Victoria Street, EC4

A recruiting poster for the Auxiliary Fire Service.

FIREFIGHTERS BRAVE THE BLITZ

Some 793 firemen and 25 firewomen lost their lives, while as many as 7,000 sustained serious injuries. Many being temporarily blinded by heat or flying sparks; and all who joined the Service were affected by the strain of working very long hours in conditions of great danger, without sleep or any regular meals, very often it was only a cup of very sweet tea from a WVS worker. It was not until the end of the Blitz, in May 1941, that Herbert Morrison, the Minister of Home Security, re-organised Britain's complicated patchwork of fire brigades into the National Fire Service.

KIDDE-GRAVINER LIMITED

DIG FOR VICTORY

THE RAILINGS OF BERKELEY SQUARE SACRIFICED FOR SCRAP

On the 10th July 1940, Lord Beaverbrook, whom Winston Churchill had made Minister of Aircraft Production, broadcast a national appeal: "Women of Britain, give us your aluminium. We want it now … we will turn your pots and pans into Spitfires, Hurricanes, Blenheims and Wellingtons. I ask therefore that anyone who has pots, pans, kettles, vacuum cleaners, hatpins, coat-hangers, shoetrees, bathroom fittings, household ornaments, cigarette boxes or other articles made wholly or partly of aluminium should hand them in at once to the local branch of the Women's Voluntary Service".

The flood of household chattels and bric-a-brac which resulted, proved to be not of high grade and of little use – leaving historic reflection to surmise whether there really was an official belief that domestic Britain harboured vast untapped sources of comparatively rare metals, when common industrial knowledge would have divulged the nature of the alloys used in household manufactures – or whether, in the greater strategy of war, it was a way of penetrating the 'phoney war' syndrome that was building up in so many minds. Whatever the raison d'etre, it was to be pursued further: hard on the great aluminium drive, followed the Iron Railings Appeal, this was actually quantified with mind-bending patriotic logic (especially in view of the mounting U-Boat activities): a half-a-million tons of railings equalled 300 new destroyers. From around squares and gardens, everywhere in fact except where the unwary in the blackout might be precipitated into the end of their war, railings were sawn or burnt off. There *were* some accusations of useless vandalism of in some cases antique artifacts (and it is indeed plain to see that the replacements were never to be the same) and it was also rumoured that the true purpose was to allow people to rush from buildings into open spaces during air raids.

In the event, by September 1944 the total weight of iron railings collected exceeded one million tons – much of which never got further than the huge rusting piles on which they were dumped.

A LONDON SHOP'S WAR

MURDER RAIDERS BOMB CHURCHES AND HOSPITALS

Read the headline in The Daily Sketch April 18, 1941. This extract came from the Jermyn Street Shop Manager's diary: On the night of Wednesday the 16th April 1941 the Dunhill shop stood intact. On Thursday night it was a mass of twisted girders, charred wood and crazy masonry. On Wednesday it was the most perfectly equipped shop in the world, encased in wonderfully patterned walnut, fitted with show cases designed to show stock of such variety and attraction that visitors exclaimed that they never had seen anything to approach it in dignity and beauty. But even bomb and fire could not put a stop to business activities.

Below: The ruins

Above: the Chairman Alfred H Dunhill calmly carries on business on the pavement in front of the ruins of his shop

NOTHING GOES TO WASTE

With supplies of raw materials limited by rationing, Mr Alfred H Dunhill recycles parts of his damaged shop by producing **'Touch Wood'** lucky charms.

DUNHILL AT DUNKIRK

It was a mammoth task of bravery spanning only 9 days from 26th May-6th June, where every seaworthy craft that could make the trip across from England to Dunkirk set out to bring back as many soldiers as their craft could carry.

Although under constant threat from the air, these brave men in their little ships continued on. One of these ships was the LADY GAY owned by Alfred Dunhill.

The LADY GAY made the trip a couple of times and performed various other duties during the conflict, proving to be a great asset to the war effort. In fact, at the start of the war Alfred Dunhill handed her over to the Royal Navy to be used as a patrol boat, where they changed her name to a number.

M.B.E. FOR SHOP MANAGER

William Carter, shop manager was entrusted with the onerous task of ensuring that all supplies of tobacco for King George VI and cigars for Winston Churchill were transmitted in top security to these illustrious and vulnerable personalities for the whole of the period of the war.

After, which in recognition for these maybe small but important special services Alfred H Dunhill was offered an MBE and he designated Carter to receive this honour.

Winston Churchill was gracious enough to ask through Lord Ismay for Carter to come to Downing Street where he shook the great man's hand and was suitably thanked.

Above: Winston Churchill with his trade mark cigar in hand standing outside Downing Street with grandson Winston.

RATIONING ...

Now a familiar scene outside the premises of Alfred Dunhill are the daily queues of military personnel together with members of the public waiting their turn to buy a famous white spot pipe

... INCIDENTALLY ...

It was in late 1940 that the Managing Director of the Danish Bacon Company (having moved its HQ to London) ordered 150 companion cases of two pipes. Each case was to be stamped with *'Four Courage and Endurance during the fight for freedom 1939-40'*. These were to be presented to the brave ship captains running the blockade to bring home the bacon to England.

... AND FINALLY ...

A day before the declaration of War an order for 1000 giant Partagas cigars was paid for in cash by the German Air Attaché in London ... the stock destined for Hermann Goering.

ALFRED DUNHILL LIMITED

HELP FOR VICTIMS OF THE BLITZ

The violent destruction of the air raid and its accompanying fires was the most
dramatic aspect of the Blitz, but equally telling was the aftermath of disruption
and inconvenience. Even the majority who left the shelters and were relieved to
find that they were not one of those whose homes had been totally destroyed or
rendered uninhabitable, invariably had to cope with everyday life bereft of the
services that had been so taken for granted, for a longer or shorter period: no
electricity or gas for lighting, cooking or heating and no water for washing or
doing any laundry – all the more essential with the clouds of dust that billowed
and permeated everything as buildings collapsed and in those adjacent, plaster
ceilings rained down.

Vital relief was provided by services such as the mobile laundries donated on
a large scale by the soap and washing-powder manufacturer Lever Brothers,
with which the victims in devastated areas could restore a semblance of
civilised comfort with clean clothes and bedding, amidst the chaos and dusty
rubble. These and other facilities such as the daily watercart and mobile
canteens to serve hot food, as necessary as medical treatment to freezing cold
people numbed with shock as they beheld their shattered streets, were carried
out by the Women's Voluntary Services – the 'WVS'. This magnificent and
dedicated effort, often under the most trying and distressing conditions, by
women across the nation was one of the most outstanding features of the war
on the Home Front. Even after mass raids, such as that on Coventry on the night
of the 14-15th of November 1940, they somehow managed to cope; not only
their material help but their very presence a great reassurance.

Organisation was another of the WVS contributions. A 'Housewives
Service' was encouraged whereby women could do their bit for their own street,
taking in bombed-out families, providing hot drinks for the often elderly Air
Raid Precaution Wardens 'ARP's', maintaining a census of residents by which
anyone missing after a raid could be identified and distributing clothing and
blankets. In the last six months of the war alone, £1.5 million of clothing,
donated by the United States and the Empire, were distributed through the
WVS.

UNILEVER PLC

The destroyer HMS Kelly steaming into action during World War II.

ROBERT TAYLOR. IN THE COLLECTION OF MR. AND MRS. ROBERT JAMES.

HMS *KELLY* – CONTACT BEARING 190

HMS *Kelly* was named after Admiral Sir John Kelly and was launched by his daughter. On 23rd August 1939, ten days before the outbreak of World War II, she was handed over by her builders, Hawthorne Leslie, to her Commanding Officer, Lord Mountbatten, who had been appointed Captain (D) commanding the 5th Destroyer Flotilla. All of the ships of the Flotilla were brand new vessels of the 'J' and 'K' Class and HMS *Kelly* was the Flotilla Leader. The Kelly was, from the first, a happy and efficient ship and the teamwork, engendered by Mountbatten, enabled the commissioning time to be cut from the usual three weeks down to three days.

One of HMS *Kelly*'s first missions was to sail to Cherbourg and return to Portsmouth, carrying the Duke and Duchess of Windsor back from France to the safety of the United Kingdom. In December 1939, Mountbatten was ordered to collect every available destroyer in the Tyne and search for a German U-Boat, which was believed to have torpedoed four ships in the River estuary. During this operation, HMS *Kelly* struck a mine, which fortunately did not explode until hit by her propellors, but she had to be towed back and repaired.

The next time that the *Kelly* was in trouble was during the Norwegian campaign, when she was ordered to intercept and sink some German minelayers. Whilst heading at full speed for her target, *Kelly* was hit by a torpedo and had to be taken in tow by HMS *Bulldog*, a destroyer from another flotilla. In spite of further attacks by both German E-Boats and the Luftwaffe, Kelly arrived home to Hawthorne Leslie's Yard at Hebburn on the Tyne after ninety-two hours in tow. HMS *Kelly* was again repaired and recommissioned in November 1940 and many of her old ship's company rejoined her.

In 1941, HMS *Kelly* was despatched to the Mediterranean and in May of that year, she sank the last of the 'caique' invasion fleet and successfully bombarded Maleme airfield in Crete. Following this action, HMS *Kelly* was herself attacked, during the Battle of Crete, by twenty-four Junkers 87 Stuka dive-bombers and turned over whilst steaming at 34 knots. More than half of the *Kelly*'s officers and men were lost and the survivors, oil-smeared and burnt, were machine gunned in the water whilst clinging to the only raft to remain afloat. Nevertheless, they still found enough voice to cheer the *Kelly* as she finally went down and Lord Mountbatten is reputed to have said: "We didn't leave the *Kelly*, the *Kelly* left us!".

The story of the *Kelly* during the first twenty-one months of the War was told by Noël Coward, a great friend of Lord Mountbatten, in his classic film "In Which We Serve". Names, places and situations were changed at Mountbatten's request, but the *Kelly*'s exploits were the inspiration for the film.

The story of HMS *Kelly* is not particularly remarkable, when set against the background of other heroic events of World War II. What singled her out was the exceptionally high morale of her ship's company under the leadership of her distinguished and respected Captain.

BIG CRATER ROYAL EXCHANGE
The Bank of England and Royal Exchange after the raid during the night of 11 January, 1941. The bomb exploded in the booking-hall of the Bank underground station. The crater, 1,800 sq.ft. in area, was the largest in London

I.W.M.

GUARDIAN ROYAL EXCHANGE plc

The Chase of Bismarck

H.M.S HOOD blows up, after a direct hit salvo from BISMARCK finds her magazines; off Greenland 25 May 1941. Photograph taken from German heavy cruiser, PRINZ EUGEN

THE BATTLESHIP 'BISMARCK'

Pride of the German navy at the start of World War II, the *Bismarck* was a mightly battleship. She had a displacement of 41,700 tons and her main armament comprised eight 15-inch guns, in four twin turrets, two fore and two aft; her secondary armament consisted of twelve 5.9-inch guns and sixteen 4.1-inch anti-aircraft guns. Although she was a floating fortress of armour plate and massive fire power, her deck armour was badly placed to deal with either bomb damage or plunging shellfire and in her last action, she very quickly succumbed to British shells.

On 21st May 1941, her Captain, Admiral Lütjens took her out of the safety of the Norwegian fjords at Bergen, into the open North Sea. Three days later, on 24th May, she was intercepted by the British Navy and during the ensuing battle, the *Bismarck* landed a direct hit on the British battleship HMS *Hood*, sinking her in one mightly explosion. Damaged herself, *Bismarck* made for St.

Nazaire for repairs, but was spotted by a Catalina flying-boat of the RAF, some 700 miles west of Brest. Shortly afterwards, Swordfish aircraft, flying from HMS *Ark Royal*, severely damaged *Bismarck*'s rudder and propellors with torpedoes, but she managed to survive the day.

The next morning, 27th May 1941, *Bismarck* was confronted by units of the Home Fleet, including the battleships HMS *Rodney* and HMS *King George V*. Unable to steer properly, the *Bismarck* fought a gallant rear guard action, but the odds against her were too great and after two hours of furious battle she was sunk by a torpedo fired from the cruiser HMS *Dorsetshire*, and went down burning from end to end. Thus ended an epic piece of Naval history. The painting depicts the *Bismarck* firing a broadside from her forward guns, during the course of her final combat.

A SHIPPING LINE AT WAR

In August 1939 the Joseph Constantine Steamship Line whose founder had first entered shipping with part-ownership of a small sailing barque in 1885, and who had lost 13 ships through enemy action in the First World War, owned a fleet of nine modern ocean-going vessels and nine coasters – all recognisable by the distinctive suffix "–wood" in their names.

The first casualty of the Line's war occurred on Christmas Eve 1939 when the EDENWOOD sank off the Nab Tower following a collision with the British Motorship Line's DERBYSHIRE whilst on a voyage from Seaham to Portsmouth with a cargo of coal. Six months later, June 1940 proved a fateful month when the BAL-MORALWOOD was torpedoed by the submarine U.47 on the 14th whilst on a voyage from Sorel to Falmouth and her equally new sister WINDSORWOOD (both being built at Newcastle-upon-Tyne in the late thirties) was sunk by U.51 en route from her home river to Sierra Leone eleven days later on the 25th, both in the North Atlantic; while in August the BROOKWOOD was torpedoed by U.37. It was the end of 1941 before the next loss, the KIRN-WOOD en route from Sydney to Ipswich, her luck having run out after surviving two previous attacks on earlier voyages. The year 1942 was a safe one for the deep sea fleet but the coasters (the 'short-sea' fleet) who were particularly liable to attack from enemy aircraft or E-Boats suffered with the LINWOOD and AVON-

SS. BRIARWOOD

WOOD being lost in November and December respectively. The New Year opened badly however when the YORKWOOD sailing home in ballast from Table Bay via Panama was sunk by U.507 whilst off the Brazilian coast and ended with the loss of the KINGSWOOD on the 17th of December 1943 in position 05.57N 01.43E in the Gulf of Guinea when she was sighted by U.515.

The ships which survived also saw action on frequent occasions. The WEARWOOD was damaged in March 1941 during an air raid on Liverpool docks and NORTHWOOD was attacked by aircraft off Whitby. The LEVENWOOD was at the evacuation of Dunkirk and the PARKWOOD had to be towed back to Plymouth after the Luftwaffe raid at Granville. As

with their human counterparts, luck seems to have espoused the cause of an individual.

Such was the amazing war of the BRIARWOOD in the thick of it. She transported men and stores to St Nazaire under attack and did the same at Narvik in Norway where she was the last British ship to leave hours before it fell to the German forces. In May 1940 she was sailing the North Atlantic unescorted when a submarine attacked her: taking skillful evasive action she avoided its torpedoes and made good her escape. A couple of days later as she neared home an aircraft made a low-level bombing run over her – and she shot it down. A few months later in July, she was bombed off Portland but managed to limp home and was repaired. At the end of that year, on the 5th of November, she was present at one of the most dramatic and courageous convoy episodes of the war at sea. The convoy she was in was intercepted by the German pocket-battleship ADMIRAL SCHEER. The escorting merchant cruiser JERVIS BAY signalled her charges to scatter while, to give them time to effect their escape, she closed with her powerful adversary and sacrificed herself in a fight to the finish. After she'd been sunk the raider located and sunk six of the ships, but again the lucky BRIARWOOD managed to slip away. In May 1942 she was the Commodore Ship of a convoy on the notorious North Russian route, with its proximity to German forces in Norway and its appaling freezing weather. The visibility during this particular voyage turned out to be very good and it suffered the attentions of five very determined German destroyers and numerous aircraft. Severe losses were suffered including the sinking of the cruiser HMS EDINBURGH but BRIARWOOD, though an obvious target in the lead, sailed through unscathed. She and the WEARWOOD were the only Constantine deep-sea ships to survive the war – the story of the line is typical of the unsung merchant sailors and their ships, who, with none of the glamour or equipment of the Forces, won their Battle in the Atlantic, and across the globe, to keep Britain from being starved of food and materials into submission.

SS. KINGSWOOD

CONSTANTINE GROUP

FRANK WOOTTON, P.G.Av.A.: In the collection of MRS A. MACCOY

WING COMMANDER TUCK SHOOTS DOWN A MESSERSCHMITT

Robert R. Stanford Tuck was a regular officer who joined the RAF in 1935, after serving a few years in the Merchant Navy. After flying training he joined No. 65 Squadron which was then equipped with Gladiators.

By December 1938, No. 65 Squadron had been re-equipped with Spitfires but although he flew with the squadron until May 1940, he saw no action with them.

He was posted in May 1940 as a flight commander to No. 92 Squadron, which also flew Spitfires, and during the heavy fighting over the Dunkirk beaches he shot down six enemy aircraft on 23 and 24 May. The next day he was slightly wounded in the thigh, the enemy bullet being stopped by a coin in his pocket. His squadron was heavily involved in the fighting over the South of England in 1940, and he had several further successes.

In early September, he was posted to command No. 257 Squadron, which flew Hurricanes, and stayed with them until July 1941, when he was posted to lead the Duxford Wing (a Wing was a unit of two to four Fighter Squadrons led by a Wing Commander). However, he was taken off operations to go to the USA in October 1941 as a member of an RAF team who demonstrated operational flying techniques to the then neutral Americans.

He returned to the British Isles in December 1941, and he was appointed to command the Biggin Hill Wing.

However, on 28 January 1942, whilst flying low on a strafing mission, his Spitfire was hit in the engine and he was forced to land, to become a prisoner of war. After many adventures, he escaped just before the war ended and made his way to the Russian lines and eventually returned to Britain. He flew in the first post-war Battle of Britain fly past in September 1945, and left the Royal Air Force shortly afterwards.

The painting shows one of his victories gained as a Wing Commander. His Spitfire carries his initials RS-T in lieu of squadron codes, a privilege of Wing Commanders (Flying) on fighter airfields during the war.

Victoria Drummond outside Buckingham Palace after receiving her MBE in July 1941. [Photo by courtesy of the Evening Standard*]*

WAR HERO FROM THE ENGINEROOM

'She is about the most courageous woman I ever saw … without fear or nerves … [she] has an uncanny power over the engines. She gets more out of the ship … than any of the others.'

That tribute was paid to Victoria Drummond, Second Engineer, by the mate of the ss BONITA in 1940, after she had single-handedly kept the ship's engines going during an attack by a German bomber, so saving the ship and the lives of the crew. It was a feat that brought her an MBE and the Lloyd's War Medal for Bravery at Sea – the first to be awarded to a woman.

A god-daughter of Queen Victoria, Victoria Drummond grew up in Megginch Castle, Perthshire, the daughter of a family with aristocratic connections. Thanks to the Great War she secured an engineering apprenticeship with a local garage, and family connections paved the way to her apprenticeship in a Dundee shipyard and helped with her first seagoing appointment with the Blue Funnel line.

She went on to become the first woman to qualify as a marine engineer in the Merchant Navy, and there is no doubt about her engineering ability. The hands-on skills gained during her apprenticeships, and an instinctive 'feel' for engines revealed by many episodes of her seagoing career, are evidence of this. When asked how she achieved her results she said, 'Oh, I just talk nicely to them. You can coax or lead engines … but you must never drive them.'

At the outbreak of the Second World War Victoria Drummond tried to secure a berth in a British ship, but prejudice stood in the way and her war service initially was as a Second Engineer in foreign-flagged ships. It was in her second ship of the war years, the Panamanian SS BONITA, that she performed the feat of courage for which she was decorated. Under heavy bombardment, she stayed alone in the engineroom amidst burst steampipes, flying debris, and terrific noise magnified by the enclosed space, coaxing an extra turn of speed out of the engines and nursing steam through a damaged pipe, by her skill giving the Captain the manoeuvrability he needed to dodge the bombs.

Dodging bombs and evading mines become part and parcel of the next five years, as did drunken crews, filthy ships and unreliable shipmates. But there were also good ships, good officers, good times and good friendships.

She was in Antwerp on VE Day and thought of the former shipmates lost at sea and the many friends lost in raids at home.

The war over, she spent the rest of her sea-going career tramping round the world in a variety of ships under foreign flags, in conditions ranging from the comfortable to the appalling. 'No one ever thought I would stick it out – but I did,' she wrote.

Sadly, she never obtained a British Chief Engineer's certificate, in spite of repeated attempts to pass the examinations, and in her later years she sailed under a Panamanian certificate. There is little doubt that prejudice played a part in this, as it did all too frequently in the reactions of some fellow seafarers, both officers and crew. But she also found much support, encouragement and companionship, and made many good friends in her years at sea.

She suffered more than her share of accident, illness and even physical assault – she once beat off three assailants in Turkey. She writes in her diaries of such episodes in a matter-of-fact way that belies the pain and also the fear that she must have felt.

Every time Victoria Drummond thought she had had enough, the lure of the sea life proved too strong. She remained at sea until well into her sixties, sailing for the last few years with Chinese owners, eventually retiring in 1962 at the age of 68, having completed 49 voyages in 40 years at sea.

The story of this skilful and courageous woman is told in a biography by her niece Cherry Drummond (Baroness Strange), who uses first-person narrative based on Victoria's own diaries, voluminous correspondence and uncompleted memoirs. Entitled *The Remarkable Life of Victoria Drummond, Marine Engineer,* it is published by The Institute of Marine Engineers, of which she was proud to be a Fellow. It can be ordered through bookshops or direct from the Institute.

BALLOONS OVER BUCKINGHAM PALACE

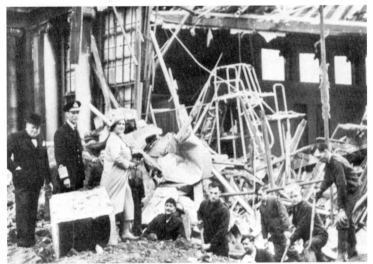

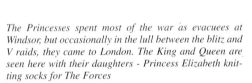

The Princesses spent most of the war as evacuees at Windsor, but occasionally in the lull between the blitz and V raids, they came to London. The King and Queen are seen here with their daughters - Princess Elizabeth knitting socks for The Forces

ABOVE: The King and Queen accompanied by Winston Churchill inspecting war damage at the Palace in September 1940.

BELOW: An artist's impression of the royal family's air-raid shelter.

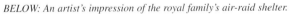

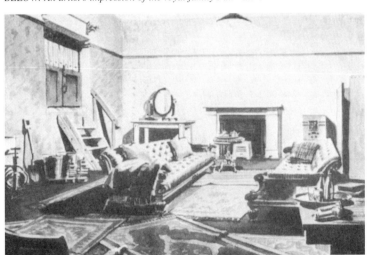

FRANK WOOTTON, P.G.AV.A.: Presented by the artist to RAF Benevolent Fund and sold to The National Air & Space Museum, Smithsonian Institution, U.S.A.

DOUGLAS BADER FAILS TO RETURN

By the time the Battle of Britain ended in October 1940 many outstanding British pilots had emerged. One of the most notable was Douglas Bader.

In 1931, he lost both his legs as a result of an aircraft crash and was medically discharged from the Royal Air Force.

By sheer courage and indomitable determination he managed to overcome this disability and he rejoined the Royal Air Force as a pilot at the outbreak of war in September 1939.

In July 1940, following service in Nos. 19 and 222 Squadrons, he was appointed to command No. 242 Squadron. This squadron had suffered heavy losses whilst fighting in France, but was soon restored to fighting efficiency by Bader's leadership.

Apart from his own success as a fighter pilot, he proved to be an outstanding air leader, as demonstrated by his leadership of up to five squadrons in the controversial "Duxford Wing" during September 1940.

In early 1941, he was promoted to Wing Commander to lead the Tangmere Wing. This was at the time Fighter Command began to take the offensive, and he led his Wing on many sweeps over enemy occupied France.

On 9th August 1941, during a sweep, he failed to return and he became a prisoner of war. Some doubt exists regarding the circumstances of his loss but it is generally thought that his Spitfire and a German fighter were in collision.

Finding himself at the controls of a tailless Spitfire, he managed to bale out, leaving one of his artificial legs in the cockpit. A replacement leg was dropped by parachute to him by the RAF during another sweep.

After many adventures, including several escape attempts, he was placed in the special Colditz Castle POW camp for would-be escapers – he was liberated just before VE-Day.

He left the RAF to become an executive in Shell Oil Company's aviation business.

He was also very active after the war in organisations connected with assisting the disabled, and by his example was an inspiration to many people, services for which he was knighted in 1976.

Sir Douglas Bader died in September 1982.

ADWEST GROUP plc   THE JANE HODGE FOUNDATION

The Blackout - Piccadilly Circus by moonlight.

The Blitz - Bedding-down in Aldwych Tube Station Shelter

HEALEY & BAKER

Search lights of 210 million candle-power probe the London night sky.

RAIDERS SEARCHED OUT

The 3.7in guns of the London barrage. At the beginning of the Blitz, when batteries were rushed to London to reinforce AA Command, many of the gun crews spent their first week in action, virtually without any sleep, catching brief moments of rest in tents with bare earth as their beds. Conditions on AA sites in the autumn of 1940 were pretty crude, the majority were clogged with mud; and the gunners lived in dug-outs, immediately beside the gun-pits; and the vibrations set up by the guns frequently collapsed and flooded them with water.

BATTLE OF SIDI REZEGH

As the war in the Western Desert swung back and forth across the 600 miles from Alexandria in Egypt to Benghazi in Cyrenaica, first against the Italian Army, and after their defeat, the Afrika Korps under General Rommel, there were many critical engagements of the most ferocious nature, marked sometimes by conduct of very personal bravery, in a warfare whose aim was to destroy the enemy, rather than occupy territory. Such an action was the great tank battle at Sidi Rezegh, in which General Cunningham, then Commander of the Eight Army attempted a counter-attack against Rommel's forces who in March 1941 had mounted a skilful and lightning attack with his superior panzer forces, in both fighting power and organisation, which had taken him to the Egyptian frontier. The battle took place on the 21st November 1941 and has rightly always been considered as one of the finest examples of bravery by individual men and a single battery.

Second Lieutenant George Gunn, Royal Horse Artillery, manned a portee 2-pounder anti-tank gun against a mass attack by German tanks, moving about his four-gun troop under the heaviest shellfire, redeploying and encouraging the men until only a sergeant and himself survived; after which be used the portee gun to engage the enemy direct. He was joined by Major Bernard Pinney, his battery commander, who succeeded in putting out the fires which were threatening the ammunition bins, and then when Gunn was killed by a direct hit, took his place in the layer's seat, maintaining a high rate of fire against the advancing tanks who were concentrating all theirs on this, the only vehicle left offering them any resistance. Another direct hit engulfed the portee in flames and Major Pinney then coolly collected up the wounded and evacuated them before joining another sector of the battle to supervise his guns there. He was killed in action the next day and like Gunn, recommended for a Victoria Cross. Sadly, Major Pinney's was only to be a Military Cross under the system which rationed awards for gallantry in any one action, and indeed sometimes even allocated them by ballot.

Above: The Port of London - warehouses and barges blaze as PLA fire-fighting craft deal with the aftermath of an air raid on St Katherine's Dock, September 1940.

Left: Liverpool Street Station the morning after a raid on the Moorgate area of the City. A large hole has been blown in the station wall and debris covers the platform; but within hours it was travel as usual, January 1941.

BANKING STAFF WAR

The Chief General Manager of the Bank placed James Greenhill in charge of the Air Raid Precautions Committee in September 1939. Mr Greenhill, who was appointed Joint General Manager of Lothbury Branch in 1933, had served as an officer in the RASC during WWI, from 1917-1919.

Plans were developed for the preservation of banking business: for the premises and for the staff who manned them. Various members of staff were allocated to specific duties, such as fire watching; service in the Home Guard; door guards, siren countrol watchmen; first aid attendants; and many other responsibilities.

At the outbreak of war, 210 staff at Lothbury were allocated to duties comprising:-

FIREMEN: 61 clerical staff, 21 messengers, 34 night cleaners.

MESSENGERS: 3 door guards, 3 siren control watchmen.

FIRST AID: 40 women, 37 men.

AIR LOCK: 11 male stewards (This was to ensure that poisinous gas did not seep into the air raid shelters constructed in the basement of Lothbury)

This rota ensured that the premises were protected at night and at weekends.

Alterations at Lothbury at the very begining of the war led to the construction of a first aid station and room; gas cleansing stations; basement seating provision and gas sealing of the lift shafts. In addition, bedding was purchased to provide emergency sleeping accomodation for those working at night in case of air raids. Meals were also provided.

£500 was spent on the purchase of respirators; suits; helments; and other equipment of the firefighting squads. These suits and asbestos gloves are shown in the photograph. (Above)

Most of the mechanised functions of banking were withdrawn from the banking hall at Lothbury and placed in the basement area, on three floors. Other banking functions, eg the Trustee Dept (which moved to Bournemouth), were evacuated to rural sites in a damage limitation exercise.

Fortunately, Lothbury did not receive any damage to its premises unlike some other City branches, eg Moorgate & Lombard Street, which received direct hits.

On 23 March 1945 all fire watching was withdrawn and the order given to restore the branch to its pre-1939 condition.

(Below) Staff firewatch members; first aid workers; and the Home Guard.

NATIONAL WESTMINSTER BANK Plc

THE 'SCHARNHORST' AND 'GNEISNAU' IN CHANNEL DASH

JOHN HAMILTON

Since mid 1941, the German battlecruisers *Scharnhorst* and *Gneisnau*, both of a standard displacement of 26,000 tons and with a primary armament of nine 11 inch guns, together with the cruiser *Prinz Eugen* had been sheltering in the French port of Brest. They had been constantly under attack by the RAF, who had dropped more than 4,000 tons of bombs on them, but had nevertheless remained afloat. Since the Germans had evidently been able to make good any damage, it was decided to try and get these important ships back to their bases.

After dark, on the night of 11th February 1942, the *Scharnhorst, Gneisnau* and *Prinz Eugen* slipped out of Brest and made a spectacular escape up the English Channel to German ports. Helped by bad weather, they had a strong escort and were protected by a huge air umbrella mounted by the Luftwaffe from shore bases, as they steamed up the Channel at a speed of about 30 knots, close to the French coast.

They were first sighted at 1100 by patrolling RAF fighters as they were approaching the narrows of the Straits of Dover. An attack was immediately launched and six Fleet Air Arm Swordfish torpedo-reconnaisance bombers of 825 Squadron, under Lieutenant Commander A. Eugene Esmonde DSO RN, flew out from the RAF Station at Manston, escorted by a large number of fighters. They attacked the enemy at mast height in the face of a furious anti-aircraft barrage and not one of the Swordfish aircraft returned. Lieutenant-Commander Esmonde was posthumously awarded the Victoria Cross, the first to be won by the Fleet Air Arm in World War II. The other four Officer survivors were each

awarded the DSO and Leading Airman Bunce the Conspicuous Gallantry Medal. The eleven members of 825 Squadron who did not return were mentioned in Despatches. Vice-Admiral B. H. Ramsey, the Flag Officer Commanding Dover, commenting on this tragic piece of human endeavour wrote: "In my opinion, the gallant sortie of these six Swordfish constitutes one of the finest exhibitions of self-sacrifice and devotion to duty that the war has yet witnessed".

As the German ships got clear of the Dover Straits and headed for their ports, Royal Navy destroyers and motor-torpedo boats carried out several attacks, but to no avail, since the enemy E-boats had laid a heavy smoke-screen. Air attacks were also kept up in great strength. However, the *Scharnhorst* and *Gneisnau* both struck mines, which had been laid ahead of them, before they finally reached their German bases.

The *Gneisnau* was severely damaged and her repairs were so constantly retarded by air attack that she took no further part in the war; being still at her berth in Lubeck when the Allies captured the port in 1945.

The *Scharnhorst* however went back to war: she was finally sunk off Norway in the battle on Boxing Day 1943 after an engagement with a squadron commanded by Admiral Sir Bruce Fraser (later C-in-C of the British Pacific Fleet, in 1945) with his flag in the battleship *Duke of York,* and which included the cruiser *Belfast,* now a floating naval museum in the Pool of London – the Battle of North Cape. *(Below: survivors of the* Scharnhorst *landing in Britain.)*

Lt.-Cdr. Eugene Esmonde VC.

TYNE TEES TELEVISION

Sergeant Thomas Parnell

THE BATTLE OF KNIGHTSBRIDGE

After the British offensive of December 1941 had foundered in the great tank battle of Sidi Rezegh, despite a preponderence of tanks, Rommel was nevertheless forced to fall back to Benghazi, then, swiftly regrouping he turned the tables in the see-saw war that was the Western Desert, and drove the Eighth Army 300 miles back to Gazala. Here the German General waited three months to regroup supplies (he flew to Germany to plead with Hitler for an invasion of Malta, the centre of interference with his supply line, which was actually promised).

By the end of May 1942 he was ready to strike at the Gazala Line, and a series of engagements ensued. One of these was the Battle of the Cauldron, fought between the 2nd and the 11th of June, the Battle of Knightsbridge, on the 6th, being part of it. 'Knightsbridge' was the name for the junction of the Bir Hacheim desert track with the Trigh Capuzzo – names familiar to the men often being used to identify key points in largely unmapped and featureless desert. It was in fact one of a series of brigade all-round defensive areas known as 'boxes'. After days of fierce fighting, the Afrika Korps broke through the British positions, very large numbers of tanks and guns being lost, despite heroic resistance. Typical was the 426th Battery of 197 Regiment Royal Horse Artillery (The South Nottinghamshire Hussars) in their gallant last stand as enemy tanks attacked them for three days; by which time they were exchanging fire at point-blank range, till their ammunition was finished and the survivors, almost all of them wounded, were forced to surrender (the Regiment is now the 100th Regiment RA, Territorial Army).

There were others in their tanks, such as Sergeant Thomas Parnell of C Squadron, 10th Royal Hussars (fifty years on, a Pensioner at The Royal Hospital, Chelsea), who recalled the confusion of the battle in his sector – and the limitations of the new Grant tanks; the 75 mm gun being so low down in the hull, rather than in its turret (which only contained a 37 mm) that before a shot could be fired a great deal of the vehicle's body had to be exposed to hostile fire.

By the 30th June, now Field Marshal, Rommel was once again in Egypt, only 60 miles from Alexandria – and the Eighth Army had fallen back on the only real defensive line in the Western Desert – El Alamein.

JOHN HAMILTON

SS OHIO REACHES MALTA – THE PEDESTAL CONVOY

In the middle of 1942, the Island of Malta was facing a desperate situation due to the tremendous pressure being put on it by the German and Italian air forces. In August of that year, "Operation Pedestal" was mounted to get a convoy of fourteen large, fast, merchant ships, carrying vital supplies, through to the Island from the west. The escorting forces included battleships, cruisers, destroyers and an aircraft carrier.

The convoy included the SS OHIO, a large, 14,000 ton tanker, belonging to the Texaco Oil Company of America, which had been chartered by the British Ministry of War Transport, especially for this convoy, to carry an exceptionally vital cargo of aviation spirit to the beleaguered Island. She was placed under the management of the Eagle Oil and Shipping Company and was manned by Captain D. W. Mason as Master and a specially selected British crew. A team of naval ratings and soldiers was also carried to man the anti-aircraft guns.

On Saturday night, 8th August, the convoy and its escort forces slipped through the Straits of Gibraltar, under the cover of darkness, and proceeded towards its destination at a speed of fiteen knots. The forenoon of the 11th August saw the first action, when the aircraft carrier HMS EAGLE was tragically sunk by a U-boat. From then on, the expected air attacks began and the convoy was under almost continuous attack by aircraft, U-boats and E-boats until it reached Malta. The OHIO was singled out for heavy attacks, and one night was hit by a torpedo and forced to stop. Steering by hand from aft, she somehow caught up with the convoy the next day. During the continuous air attacks concentrated against the OHIO, the ship was straddled by a stick of bombs, which almost lifted her out of the water. Eventually, a bomb exploded in her boiler room and she was again brought to a stop. Temporary repairs were

achieved and the OHIO struggled on. A Stuka dive-bomber aircraft shot out of control and crashed on her deck. She was once more hit by a bomb, which put the engines out of action and she was then taken in tow. Twice she was abandoned and twice re-boarded. However, the end of this long drawn-out ordeal was approaching and British aircraft from Malta were beginning to provide air cover, but she was not home yet!

At dawn on 14th August, a near miss carried away the SS OHIO'S rudder and holed her aft, but with two destroyers either side and one ahead she was got underway again. While the AA gunners aboard the tanker and the destroyers fought off the divebombers, the crew worked desperately to keep the ship afloat. As Malta came in sight, naval tugs came out to give assistance to the gradually sinking ship. As day dawned on 15th August, the SS OHIO was literally carried into Valetta harbour between two destroyers, where she received a tremendous welcome. When the last of her precious cargo was pumped out, she settled down on the bottom of the harbour.

Operation Pedestal enabled Malta to survive and regain her critically important position in the Mediterranean. Five of the fourteen merchant ships in the convoy reached Malta, but in spite of the loss of HMS EAGLE the cruisers HMS MANCHESTER and HMS CAIRO and a destroyer, a heavy toll was taken on the enemy submarines and E-boats.

Captain D. W. Mason, Master of the OHIO, was awarded the George Cross, in recognition of his personal courage and determination and that of every member of his crew. In 1946, the hulk of the OHIO was towed out of Valetta harbour and sunk in deep water off Malta – a fitting burial ground for such a great ship.

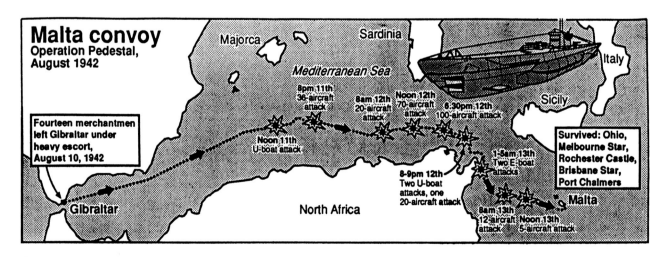

TEXACO

AIR VICE MARSHAL N. E. HOAD, C.V.E., C.B.E., A.F.C., RAF Rd.

PATROLLING SUNDERLAND FLIES AN ATLANTIC CONVOY PATROL

A Royal Air Force Sunderland flying boat patrols with a convoy in the distance. Sunderland crews thought very highly of their aircraft, and the sight of one of these large aircraft was always most welcome to men on board ships in the North Atlantic during the war.

Developed just before the war from the Short "Empire" class passenger flying boats, the Short Sunderland first entered RAF service in 1938.

Apart from its offensive armament of depth charges for use against enemy submarines, the Sunderland was well equipped to look after itself, as it featured power operated nose and tail turrets, and the later Mark 3 also had a power operated dorsal turret. This heavy defensive armament earned the nickname "The Flying Porcupine" from German aircrews opposed to the Sunderland.

Sunderland crews flew many hours in terrible weather on anti-submarine patrols over the North Atlantic, often without seeing any sign of an enemy U-boat. When a submarine was sighted, the action was often brief and violent; the submarine usually dived as quickly as possible leaving the Sunderland to attack only the "swirl" left on the surface by the diving U-boat. From 1943 onwards, the submarines began to mount multiple 37mm and 20mm cannons in their conning towers, and if the U-boat commander chose to stay on the surface and fight it out, the Sunderland was extremely vulnerable to the U-boat's AA fire. A number were lost in these circumstances, and the forward firing armament was enhanced to deal with surfaced U-boats' gunners.

Caught on the surface.
JOHN HAMILTON. Copyright, MRS BETTY HAMILTON

VAUX GROUP plc

55

I.W.M.

RED CROSS NURSING & HOME FRONT WORKERS

Farringdon Market 1945 after a V-2 attack.

Tea-time for run down women Civil Defence workers, convalesing in the home of a former Cabinet Minister. The house is situated in a well-known London Square; and is supervised by Red Cross and St. Johns nurses.

THE BOOTS COMPANY PLC

Churchill's underground domain – the Cabinet War Rooms, with the designers: Major General Sir L C Hollis KBE and Mr L F Burgis CVO CMG.

Winston Churchill's desk.

I.W.M.

In a disused tunnel of London's underground, 150 part-time workers, men and women members of the LPTB staff, nightly make munitions. They clock out of their regular job at 4.30pm and start their war work at 5pm.

LONDON TUBE STAFF PART-TIME WORK

I.W.M.

Tube shelters being entertained, during the Blitz, by George Formby, who lead the first concert party to arrive in Normandy after D-Day.

ROYAL ORDNANCE Plc   LONDON TRANSPORT

EL ALAMEIN

Commencing on the 23rd October 1942, the Battle of El Alamein was to prove the decisive turning point of the Second World War. It was to presage the eventual total defeat, seven months later, of all Axis forces in North Africa: obviating the threat to Britain's Middle Eastern oil interests and the Suez Canal and providing a springboard for an invasion of southern Europe which was the end of Italy's war and the beginning of the process that culminated with victory in Germany itself.

The turning point, decreed, as so much else in war, by intervening fate, in the career of unknown 55 year old General Bernard Law Montgomery had been back in early August when the new commander selected for the Eighth Army, General Gott, had been killed in an air accident en route to Egypt and Montgomery, hastily asked to substitute. He took over command of forces that, having defeated the Italian Tenth Army back in 1941 to surrender, had since been outmanoeuvred and out-generalled, both tactically and strategically, by the German Afrika Korp commanded by a man of genius in mechanised warfare, Rommel, in the see-saw battles that had taken place on a Front that moved over 600 miles from Alexandria in Egypt to Benghazi in Cyrenaica. Under the new Commander-in-Chief, General Alexander, he set about re-equipping the Eighth Army both morally and materially. On 31st August he merely repulsed an attack by Rommel at Alam Haifa, foregoing the advantages of following it

up as with a Wellingtonian carefulness he waited till the logistics of equipment and planning preparation were at odds overwhelmingly in his favour, with Rommel starved in favour of the German High Command's pre-occupation with the Eastern Front, and the Army rebuilt with a steady flow of reinforcements, including the new American Sherman tank, more of a match for the German panzers' Tiger machines, the time was right: outnumbering their tanks five-to-one and troops four-to-one. With strange echoes of the Great War, it opened with a 1,000 gun bombardment, a breakthrough of fixed defensive lines was achieved and a mobile tank dog-fight engaged, more reminiscent of war at sea, where the object was to destroy the enemy, not occupy territory. During this fierce action the 2nd Battalion The Rifle Brigade, supported by 239 Battery Royal Artillery with only 6-pounder anti-tank guns withstood relentless attacks by the German armour, accounting for some 32 tanks. Lt Col V. B. Turner winning the V.C. Deceived by a feint into believing the final thrust was against his northern flank, Rommel was wrong-footed when Montgomery broke through against the Italians two miles to the south; and after twelve days' intense fighting the Afrika Korps began to withdraw and the 'Desert Rats' began the long drive, for the last time, along the coast road: Sidi Barrani, Tobruk, Gazala, Benghazi to the Mareth Line in Tunis – and finally the surrender of a quarter of a million Axis prisoners at Cap Bon in May 1943.

British troops marching into Tobruk. This strongly fortified the town, of which the Germans made such a song when they captured it in June, fell to the British troops without a shot being fired.

UNION JACK HOISTED OVER TOBRUK

The Union Jack is hoisted in Tobruk in place of the swastika. The British tommy stands symbolically, on the swastika as he hauls the Union Jack up into the breeze.

NORTH AFRICA – MAJOR H W (PAT) LE PATOUREL, VC

On the 3rd of November 1942, after twelve days of intense fighting which, with stubborn German resistance, assumed an attrition quality reminiscent of the First World War, Rommel realised that Montgomery's Eighth Army had won the battle centred on El Alamein (though neither of them could have remotely perceived that this would subsequently be seen as the turning point of the war itself in the Allies' favour). The German General's withdrawal was too quick for the tanks that wheeled north to trap the Afrika Korps, but the retreat of his now severely depleted forces was headlong, as the Eighth Army pounded in pursuit up the familiar coastal road through Sidi Barrani, Tobruk, Gazala and Benghazi battlefields, seen for the last time as the Germans withdrew right to the Tunisian border. Meanwhile, on the 9th of November an Anglo-American force under General Eisenhower landed in Morocco and Algeria, the British component being General Anderson's First Army of which the 78th Division spearheaded the initial landings, then made a dash along the coast from Algiers in an attempt to reach Tunis. But the Division's progress was soon halted as they became involved in bitter fighting with paratroopers, as the Germans poured reinforcements into Tunisia in an effort to support Rommel.

By the 3rd of December 1942 the 2nd Battalion The Hampshire Regiment had been locked in combat for three days at the Tebourba Gap. At 11.00 hours on the fourth day the enemy launched an attack on all the positions still held by the now depleted 2nd Battalion, concentrating their heaviest fire on the Battalion's left flank. After about an hour the Germans had secured the high ground and brought heavy machine-gun fire to bear. The situation looked hopeless. Major Le Patourel decided to launch one last desperate attack to clear the enemy from their commanding position. His brave action was to win him the Victoria Cross.

The citation read:

"This officer personally led four volunteers under very heavy fire to the top in a last attempt to dislodge several enemy machine-guns. The party was heavily engaged by machine-gun fire and Major Le Patourel rallied his men several times and engaged the enemy, silencing several machine-gun posts. Finally, when the remainder of his party were all killed or wounded, he went forward alone with a pistol and some hand-grenades to attack enemy machine-guns at close quarters, and from this action he did not return. Major Le Patourel's most gallant conduct and self-sacrifice, his brilliant leadership and tenacious devotion to duty in the face of a determined enemy were beyond praise." It was believed that Le Patourel had been killed, and in fact his Victoria Cross was awarded 'posthumously' – but later it was discovered that he had been seriously wounded and taken prisoner.

ALLIED-LYONS PLC

While heavy winter rains held up any advance, on Tunis' further east the Eighth Army took Tripoli and approached the Mareth Line on the southern Tunisian border. On the 17th February Rommel broke through the Us II Corps but was forestalled by a gallant stand by the 1st Guards Brigade and the 26th Armoured at the Kasserine Pass. He then threw his main weight of three armoured divisions against Montgomery at Medenine, but the latter's anti-tank defences were too strong and the attack failed.

On the 20th of March the Eighth Army assaulted the Mareth Line and after some heavy fighting and an audacious flanking move, the now battered German forces fell back to Enfidaville. On the 7th of May the 7th Armoured entered Tunis and on the 11th the remaining Axis forces, trapped in the Cap Bon Peninsula, surrendered. A quarter of a million prisoners were taken and the war in North Africa had been brought to a triumphant conclusion.

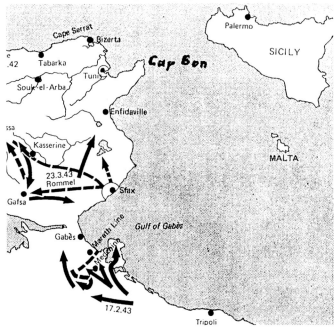

SUSTAINING FORWARD

Prior to the Second World War, feeding soldiers could perhaps, kindly have been described as "adequate". Each Regiment had its own cooks, few of whom had volunteered for cooking duties. In 1937 Leslie Hore Belisha; Secretary of State for War, invited Sir Isadore Salmon, to become Honorary Catering Adviser to the Army. As a result of Sir Isadore's recommendations in the "Salmon Report", improvements to army messing was initiated. Two years and nine months later the Army Catering Corp was formed by Special Army Order 35 of 1941.

THE DAILY WATERCART

The Western Desert, queueing up with all kinds of carriers to get their water, there is ample for the men, but a lot is used during the hot weather, so that the suppliers are kept busy.

PORTALS GROUP plc

Make your Food Budget go Further with

HP SAUCE

H.P. Sauce will help you to use up every scrap of meat, fish, vegetables, etc. H.P. improves all roasts and grills, savouries and made-up dishes. Here is one excellent recipe :—

BAKED EGG BELFORT

Cut the tops of some large tomatoes and scoop out insides. Half fill with chopped cold meat mixed with a teaspoonful of H.P. Sauce. Add tiny piece of butter or margarine. Break an egg into each. Stand on greased tin and bake in moderate oven.

COI

HP JOINS THE FIGHT

The evacuation area of Birmingham included Aston, so, with young men being conscripted, many of the HP employees found their families sadly depleted. Eventually only the highly skilled technicians at HP were excused from being called-up. Once more as in the Great War of 1914-18, married women stepped into the breach and returned to the Sauce factory, where for their safety a basement had been converted into an air-raid shelter.

During the years of war HP did not neglect its duties, the workforce became fire fighters, air-raid wardens, and formed their own Home Guard company. Their biggest responsibility was to cope with the demand for the Sauce from both the armed forces and the civilian population. The uncertain availability of raw materials and the priority of supplying the troops meant that HP was often hard to find in certain parts of the country. But a wise housewife made quite sure there was one bottle in the larder.

RABBIT PIE

1 rabbit
¼ lb scraps of bacon or pork
1 teaspoonful chopped parsley
pinch of herbs
salt and power
stock or water
short pastry

Joint the rabbit and wash it well. As we've said before, we always leave the rabbit in salted water for an hour to make certain it's quite clean. You can't be too particular abut this. Put it in a pie-dish with the other things, seasoning it well with salt and pepper. Add a little stock or water, cover with the pastry – you know how – and bake two to two-and-a-half hours

From Gert and Daisy's Wartime Cookery Book.

WHAT FISH? PIE

1 lb any white fish
2 lb hot mashed potatoes
3 tbs HP Sauce
salt and pepper
½ pt water

Place fish in salted water, cook 10min. When cooked remove bones, flake fish. Mix fish with HP Sauce, add pepper, place in dish. Put mashed potatoes on top. Brown under the grill until the top is golden. Add fish water to a little HP Sauce, for the gravy.

LORD WOOLTON'S VEGETABLE PIE

The chef of the Savoy Hotel created a dish called Lord Woolton's Vegetable Pie. Some Liverpudlians believe that Lord Woolton favoured this recipe because of his connection with their city, which has a meatless stew called Blind Scouse traditionally eaten on Bally Ann Day (the day before pay day). Scouse is 'Liverpool' for stew. Ordinary Scouse is a stew of meat and vegetables. Unlike Lord Woolton's Pie, Scouse doesn't have a crust.

1lb potatoes
1 lb cauliflower
1 lb swedes
1 lb carrots
3 or 4 spring onions
1 teaspoon vegetable extract
1 tablespoon oatmeal
chopped parsley
wheatmeal pastry (or extra potatoes) for crust

Cook the first 7 ingredients together for 10 minutes with just enough water to cover. Stir occasionally to prevent sticking. Allow to cool, put into a pie-dish, sprinkle with chopped parsley and cover with a crust of wheatmeal pastry or potato. Bake in a moderate oven until the pastry is nicely browned and serve hot wtih a brown gravy. This mixture of ingredients might be varied in many ways that may suggest themselves to the cook.

HP FOODS LIMITED

THE ANSWER TO RATIONING – EATING OUT

The great increase in communal eating partly compensated for the limitations of rationing. For instance, the number of industrial and commercial canteens soared from some 1500 in 1939 to over 18,500 by 1944. These places were accorded extra allowances of meat, cheese, butter and sugar per meal (the best of all were those that catered for 'heavy' workers: they received twice the norm) and, parents, the vast majority of whom worked and had access to the canteens, also were able to deploy far more of their ration allowances on the children in this way. And war created another first – a nationalised industry in the midst of a very private sector: the 'British Restaurants' run by local authorities and subsidised by the Ministry of Food. By September 1943, over 2000 were spread across the country, mainly in the urban areas, serving some 600,000 meals per day – all at 1s (5p) each! They were virtually the first time that the labour-saving self-service system (with everything collected on the customer's tray and paid for at an end-of-the-line cashier) had been seen in a Britain that pre-war had had plenty of low-cost labour only too eager to do this job.

Apart from this more 'institutionalised' eating out, there was a huge increase in more normal venues. In 1939 the Grenada cinema Chain had twelve restaurants employing 82 staff to serve 250,000 meals per year. Three outlets closed after the war started and the management must have felt the business was in for lean times, but they were wrong – by 1945 the nine remaining employed 216 staff dealing with 1.5 million meals per year.

Throughout the war, however, a first class meal could still be had if the diner was prepared or able to pay enough for it. At first, customers were enjoying an artificial ceiling as, even in 5-star venues, couverts were restricted to one main course at a maximum charge of 5s (25p) – till that sum was eventually abolished for 'superior' restaurants, whether by influential lobbying or in a gesture to punish the bon viveurs, resulting in sharp practices and soaring prices at these establishments (terrible things happened, such as a bill for £10 for a meal for three at a world famous Mayfair hotel!)

A 'picnic lunch', served from a mobile canteen of The American Committee for Air Raid Relief to Great Britain; shortly after a V-bomb strike, and below: a works canteen.

HILLSDOWN HOLDINGS PLC

TIME TO RELAX - ABOVE AND BELOW

ABOVE: Wrens engage theirselves in torpedo maintenance; while the crew look on relaxing, leaning over the rail at their hard work.
BELOW: Submariners take time off to have a 'Wills' smoke, a meal and catch up on the news in the papers.

IMPERIAL TOBACCO LIMITED

Great Tower Street

A COMPANY AT WAR

By the 1930's, the great merchant adventuring companies whose business had been the very raison d'etre for the British Empire, exporting finished goods to the most far-flung and perilous corners of the world and bringing back the raw materials on which an ever-diversifying industrial economy depended, and whose exploits were often the stuff of adventure and heroics, must have believed their tumultuous days to be history.

Typical was Harrisons & Crosfield, nearing their centenary. Instead, Dunkirk saw one of their companies, Paul's, grain-carrying barges in the evacuation, three out of five being lost, then first their Manchester followed by their London premises being bombed out in 1940; and in 1941 their Ipswich silo and warehouses. Meanwhile another member of the Group, Wilkinsons, was able to apply their rubber latex invention 'Linatex' to leak and flameproof RAF fuel tanks after a shot-down German aircraft had revealed that secret. On the 10th of May 1941 the Group's headquarters at 1 Gt Tower Street in the City was gutted by incendiary bombs, leaving an otherwise intact building bereft of all furniture and records – except a scorched Minute Book which miraculously survived. To spread further risk, operations were moved to two London outskirts: Nothwood in Middlesex and Epsom in Surrey, billets being found for office staff (predominantly now female, with the men in the forces) nearby to enable this vital supplier of raw materials to the war effort to continue operations.

It at least saved the logistical nightmare of reaching the City by Blitz disrupted transport. Sir Eric Macfadyen, H&C's noted Estates Manager and a recognised authority on tropical agriculture, described how, leaving his Meopham Bank home in Kent, he took a steam shuttle-train to Sevenoaks, electric tram to Knockholt, bus to Orpington, another train to Catford Bridge, bus to Lewisham and a final electric train to London Bridge to get to work.

Meanwhile the Group's Far Eastern rubber, tea and timber plantations in Malaya, Sumatra, Java, Borneo and Singapore were literally a world away. A record rubber crop in 1939 enjoyed the high London Commodities price of 10s 6p per pound; and the prewar market regulatory production quotas were abolished. That year, the Group's pre-tax profit was £345,000. And although this halcyon state of affairs in the sunshine was of course tempered by concern at the news from home and Europe that percolated throughout 1940, the only real problem was the U-Boat threat to the now burgeoning vital raw materials lifeline to Britain. those perceptive few who ventured to wonder about an obviously macho Japan were referred to the fact that Singapore itself was an impregnable fortress to the only approach for any invader – from the sea; and the 'impenetrable' jungles of Malaysia were that region's unbreachable land defence. But as 1941 ended, so did these convictions – on the 7th of December, as Pearl Harbour was attacked, Hong Kong and the Philippines were invaded.

As the now amazed and horrified expatriates watched, from far-flung plantation and city, Japanese forces landed in Southern Thailand and Northern Malaysia on the 10th of December – a day that historians have since pinpointed as the very moment of the end of the legend, and the natives belief in, the Imperial white man's invincibility: it also witnessed a Far Eastern race sink both the 'Prince of Wales' and the 'Repulse' – the technological symbols of that erstwhile supposed superiority. The Planters' families, many unknowingly being parted forever, were evacuated from their wide verandahed bungalow homes to Australia and India, the men joining the British forces, falling back from Malaysia on Singapore (from where in the event only one or two individuals would escape internment). At the Group's Batu Caves factory for Linatex, machinery was dismantled and production moved to South India. Penang fell on the 18th of December, just before a last phrenetic Far Eastern Christmas with its cottonwool 'snow' everywhere, then Kuala Lumpur on 11 January 1942. On the 7th of February the British community in Singapore assembled for Sunday lunch at Raffles, as they'd done ever since the 'Emergency' had been recognised, to listen to the BBC and talk – and the next Sunday General Percival surrendered the colony to Lieutenant-General Yamashita.

Just before that, a local doctor had driven his Daimler over a quayside into the water and then seen his wife off on the last flyingboat to leave for Australia.

Out in the jungles of Sumatra, other Planters awaited the inevitable – and it came. One I R Mathieson, recalled: "I was accosted by the first Japanese soldier to reach the estate. He was fairly friendly. He asked where my wife was! I was indeed glad she'd gone! He then asked about my car (which had been immobilised) and sent a crowd of Bataks to fetch it. They could do nothing with it, so he took my wristwatch and left. Looking at the sword and revolver by his side I hadn't felt inclined to argue. I phoned George Cameron on Simbolon Estate only to be cut off immediately it was answered; so I went round via back-roads on a motor cycle that I'd hidden. It was the first time I'd ever seen the large bungalow in eerie dark quiet, I avoided going in and searching round. Eventually I found the office guard and Cameron's driver squatting near the garage in a dazed state. Slowly they told me that a group of Jap soldiers had arrived about midday marched the three Europeans to a ravine and shot them. Bruce and Cameron's bodies were still there, but Campbell had survived and got back to the house where he changed his blood-stained clothing. They had last seen him heading purposefully south through the tea plantation; in fact his body was found later, dead from parang (a machete) wounds – certainly not inflicted by the Japanese.

All the British and Dutch staff were interned. The unlucky ones ended up building the Burma railway an experience which few survived. Others were concentrated under guard in a descending scale of 'comfort' – first in a hospital, then a school, then a native prison. Eventually they were put to work on rubber estates – but, amazingly, not tapping that product for the Japanese war effort but clearing them to grow sweet seed potatoes, maize and rice; or at hard labour repairing airfields and other installations that some of the very same men had all too efficiently destroyed as a denial tactic, when the invasion was imminent.

In London, Harrisons & Crosfield 'celebrated' their centenary wondering about the fate of hundreds of their staff with nineteen offices and all the plantations in enemy hands. And planning began for a postwar period that nobody had any idea of the advent of; the shortages of materials, staff and shipping space that would be certain; as well as an analysis of the lessons to be learnt for an international company – the most obvious one being never to be so dependent on one geographical area.

In August 1945, one Glasspool, the internees' spokesman, was suddenly advised by the Japanese that the meagre ration of a bowl of rice, maize and one sweet-potato was to be doubled. A week later distant cheering carried across the jungle from a Filipino camp, they wondered but didn't dare to hope; then on 23 August the daily six am parade was told by the Japanese commander that they were being given a day's holiday – but at eight am they had to fall in again: this time Glasspol stood alone to tell them that the Japanese had advised him that the war was over. All the released internees were sent home for recuperative leave as soon as passages could be found, and then the enormous job of reconstructing the firm began.

Fifty years on, a diversified truly worldwide group has a market value of more than £1 billion.

HARRISONS & CROSFIELD plc

IWM

For a healthy, happy job

Join the
**WOMEN'S
LAND
ARMY**

APPLY TO NEAREST W.L.A COUNTY OFFICE OR TO W.L.A HEADQUARTERS 6 CHESHAM PLACE LONDON S.W.1 STREET

WOMEN TAKE OVER THE JOBS OF THE MEN
To release the men folk for the more arduous duties of warfare, women took over many of the jobs, including bus conductors, postwomen etc.
One of the first women milk saleswomen, seen driving her horse round the streets, was Mrs Coombs of West Norwood, July 1940.

EXPRESS DAIRY

RANGE AND VISION – OPTRONICS' WAR ROLE

Barr & Stroud, the famous Glasgow firm, now part of Pilkington Optronics, was founded by two young university professors, Archibald Barr and William Stroud, in 1888. During the First World War their rangefinders went into action on land and sea and in 1917 its first submarine periscope. At the outbreak of war in 1939 it was already established as Britain's leading manufacturer of precision optical instruments, with a workforce of 2000 which was to grow to 6100 by 1944. With warfare now much more sophisticated, the firm was inundated with orders for the high technology optical instruments essential, and shadow factories had to be rapidly commissioned. The firm supplied a total of 26,650 of 1-metre-base FT37 rangefinders to the British Army, which saw action on all the battlefields: typical was the Battle of Monte Casino in Italy in 1944, "we were held up by a nest of concealed mortars – my B & S rangefinder gave 375.5 yards and setting my sights by it, I was able to hit a pile of shells, which exploded, taking the position out completely." At the request of the Ministry of Supply the Company gave invaluable help to both American and Canadian manufacturers of rangefinders and heightfinders.

The RAF relied on Barr & Stroud to supply tens of thousands of gunsights and bombsights throughout the war. Over 5000 course-setting Mark IX were supplied till Bomber Command adopted the revolutionary gyro-stabilised Mark XIV; and over 80,000 sights were fitted to the guns in the bombers' turrets. The Reflector Sight GM2 was the standard fighter pilots' equipment, used to deadly effect throughout the Battle of Britain, and also by the US Eighth Air Force; 65,000 being delivered.

The Anniesland firm's largest sphere of activity, as in 1914, was the Royal Navy. The naval range finder was still a major product line in 1939, even though since 1935 when the British scientist R Watson Watt had first demonstrated it, RADAR had begun to supersede it. This was because though the Navy received its first Type 79 sets actually in September 1939, they were prone to breakdown and interference and the masts on which their key was mounted vulnerable to blast damage. Clearly a sophisticated fighting ship could not be left totally dependent on the new weapon. Battleships continued to carry up to seventeen optical rangefinders – and they were absolutely vital in crucial and historical engagements throughout the war: on the 24th of May 1941 the battle-cruiser 'Hood' and the newly completed battleship 'Prince of Wales' engaged the German battleship 'Bismarck' and the heavy-cruiser 'Prince Eugen'.

The 'Prince of Wales' had gunnery radar which broke down; and she was refused permission to turn on her search radar, as a substitute, on the grounds that it would interfere with the 'Hood's set. With heavy seas forward she had to rely on only a 15 foot range finder in the after DCT, but at 15,000 yards her sixth salvo straddled 'Bismarck' before 'Hood' sustained several hits and blew up. And in the final engagement with 'Bismarck' the 'King George V' had to switch to her optical rangefinder, instead of radar. On Boxing Day 1943 the battleship 'Duke of York' opened fire on the battle-cruiser 'Scharnhorst', in the Battle of North Cape, using her rangefinder because the clutter from heavy weather made her radar unusable: she straddled her target with her first salvo in an action that eventually saw the German warship sunk.

Barr & Stroud delivered over 75,000 CF41 and CF42 binoculars to the Admiralty during the war – excellent for night conditions – as participants in the Battle of Metapan, when three Italian cruisers and three destroyers were sunk in the Mediterranean darkness, testified. But one of the firm's most essential contributions was to provide the 'eyes' of the Silent Service – all 215 of His Majesty's submarines relying on its periscopes. A submarine periscope usually contains over twenty air-glass surfaces and since light suffers a transmission loss of 5 per cent on each, brightness at the eye-piece was seriously impaired. The company devised a coating of magnesium fluoride two-hundred-thousandth of an inch thick, deposited in an ultra-high vacuum, as the solution. They also invented an 'air-blast' system to clear sea spray from the 'window'. In September 1943, six X-craft midget submarines, each with a crew of four men and carrying two explosive charges, had to be equipped with periscopes – in this case only nine feet in length with a 0.6 inch external tube: a feat of miniaturisation. The craft were towed to Norway to attack the battleship 'Tirpitz' at anchor in Altenfjord; three of them managed to drop their charges beneath her, inflicting considerable damage, the operation earning two Victoria Crosses – typical of the many actions throughout the war which would not have been possible without the *eyes* of Barr & Stroud.

WING COMMANDER GUY GIBSON LEADS THE DAMBUSTERS

An aircraft type is often associated with one operation which managed to catch the public eye.

No example is more typical than the linking of the Lancaster and the raid on the Ruhr Dams on 16/17 May 1943. Historically the attack was one of those which formed part of the "Battle of the Ruhr" in 1943.

It had been long recognised that modern industrial processes require many tons of water, none more so that those processes required to make high grade steel.

Dr Barnes Wallis had calculated the amount of high explosive required to break these huge concrete and earth structures. No aircraft yet built could carry a load large enough to accomplish this, but successive bombs delivered accurately at the same spot could succeed.

Bomber Command formed No. 617 Squadron under the command of Wing Commander Guy Gibson to carry out such an operation.

He was, unusually, given a free hand to select the best crews available in No. 5 Group, and the squadron set up its base at Scampton. A period of intense training was required. The weapon, a cylindrical bomb designed by Barnes Wallis, was designed to bounce over the surface of the water until it struck the dam, and then to sink until it reached a predetermined depth, when pressure fuses would explode it.

Nineteen aircraft of No. 617 Squadron carried out the attack on the night of 16/17 May. Very precise flying was required in terms of speed and height, which made the Lancasters ideal targets for the defending light AA guns at the Mohne.

Gibson attacked first, but after the second Lancaster was shot down, he flew alongside each of the other attackers, flashing his lights and drawing off the defending AA fire. The painting shows Gibson in Lancaster AJ-G (the further aircraft) during this phase of the attack. For his gallantry and leadership he was awarded the Victoria Cross.

Two dams were breached, but the operation cost No. 617 Squadron dearly. Of the nineteen aircraft despatched, eight failed to return, including those flown by both flight commanders. The squadron remained in being after the action as a specialist precision bomber unit and was later involved, with No. 9 Squadron, in the sinking of the Tirpitz. The squadron has been known within the Royal Air Force ever since 1943 as "The Dambusters".

THE BERNARD SUNLEY TRUST

KING GEORGE VI VISITS DAMBUSTER SURVIVORS AND THEIR GROUNDCREW

His Majesty was much moved by the reports of the raid and visited 617 squadron soon afterwards.

Two Lancasters have been drawn up in line, and in front of them is a file of ground crew of the squadron. (Note that none of the airmen is wearing an air-crew brevet, and all are dressed, in RAF terminology, in their "best blue").

The Avro Lancaster entered squadron service in early 1942, having been developed from the Manchester. This aircraft had two Rolls-Royce Vulture engines which had suffered from a series of troubles. Accordingly, the Manchester was redesigned with four Rolls-Royce Merlins, and was immediately successful. All versions of the Lancaster except the Mark II version used the famous Rolls-Royce engine, including two versions which used Merlins built by the Packard Motor Co in the USA.

The Mark II Lancaster used four Bristol Hercules engines, which were chosen in case the supply of Merlins was endangered.

The Lancaster I and III were identical, except that the Mark III used Packard built Merlins. It was not unknown for a Mark I to become a Mark III, and vice versa, following an engine change, such was the standardisation achieved. The other major production variant was the Mark X, built in Canada, and powered with Packard built Merlins.

The total production of Lancasters was 7,366, including over 400 in Canada, which were used by the RCAF squadrons of Bomber Command.

Avro Lancaster
Span: 102ft 0in
Length: 69ft 6in
Speed: 287 mph at 11,500 feet
Engines: (all except Mark II variant) 4 x Rolls-Royce Merlins

RACAL ELECTRONICS Plc   RHP BEARINGS LTD

HALIFAX "S-SUGAR"

The Handley Page Halifax was the second four-engined bomber to be used by the RAF, first operating with No. 35 Squadron on 10 March, 1941. Early on, the need to fit much extra equipment caused a sharp increase in all-up weight and by mid-1942 the problems were becoming serious. Consequently the nose turrets were removed, and mid-upper turrets altered and other modifications made to reduce drag. The shape of the fins was also changed to improve handling.

Finally in the Marks Three and Six, the Merlin engines were exchanged for Bristol Hercules radials and the tail wheels made retractable. The much improved Mark Threes entered service with front-line bomber squadrons late in 1943.

The aircraft depicted here, W1048 was originally issued to No. 102 Squadron and then transferred in early April 1942 to No. 35 Squadron where it became "S-Sugar". On 27 April, 1942, with 31 other Halifaxes, it took off to bomb the German battlship Tirpitz in a Norwegian fjord. The aircraft was hit by flak and the starboard wing set on fire. The pilot, Flying Officer Donald MacIntyre, tried to reach neutral Sweden some 40 miles away but as the fire took hold, he was forced to belly-land the aircraft on the frozen Lake Hoklingen. Eventually the wreckage broke through the ice and sank into the mud some 90 feet down. All seven members of the crew survived although the flight-engineeer suffered a foot injury.

The six who were uninjured evaded the German search parties and three days later reached neutral Sweden. But Sgt Vic Stevens, the injured flight engineer was taken prisoner when he elected to remain behind in Norway rather than jeopardise his comrades' chances of escape.

Thirty years later, the aircraft was recovered in a remarkably good state of preservation by an RAF and civilian salvage team and was brought back to Great Britain for display in the RAF Museum. This painting, now on show at Hendon, depicts the crew of "S-Sugar" receiving last minute instructions before taking off on the fateful flight.

HALIFAX BUILDING SOCIETY

TUNIS......VICTORY CELEBRATIONS

IWM

A Victory parade was held in Tunis on 20 May 1943, when units from the Allied Forces marched through the town. All the Allied Commanders were present and a salute at the March past was taken by General Eisenhower, General Alexander, General Anderson and General Giraud.

A cartoon of the war years by Cartoonist Acanthus, which sends Mrs Miniver and Vera Lynn into the attack in North Africa.

"You, Daisy Perkins, will lead the attack, supported by Mrs. Miniver and Vera Lynn."

LOW & BONAR Plc

NORFOLK, SUFFOLK AND 'THE MIGHTY EIGHTH'

Though the first American troops landed at Belfast on 26th January 1942 and 'The Allies' became a reality, the part played by that country had been an ever-increasing one since the outbreak of war. First there were the volunteers who did everything from flying in the Battle of Britain to ferrying aircraft. Then Winston Churchill's famous address in February 1941 exhorted his audience there to "Give us the tools and we will finish the job", paving the way for President Roosevelt to get his Lend-Lease legislation through Congress one month later, giving him the power to lease or lend material and services to any nation whose defence he considered in the interests of United States security.

It was on the wide flat spaces of Norfolk and Suffolk that the American contribution in the first half of the war in Europe became such a great, and in every way high profile, reality. The two counties reverberated to the roar of Pratt & Witney engines, as wing after wing of the United States Eighth Air Force flew in the output of that great economy's mass-production aircraft factories. Soon the new bomber bases became 'Little Americas' with their hamburgers, hot-dogs, icecream and a whole range of transatlantic food, far-removed from the local homely experience; not to mention the PXs on which to deploy their significantly higher pay: stocked with equally unknown imported goodies such as Camels, Chesterfield and Lucky Strike (3d for 20), nylon stockings, Hershey bars, all manner of canned foods and the ubiquitous chewing-gum in many brands.

Soon the dawn skies were shared with the rooks by ever bigger and bigger flights of the bombers on their few minutes to the coast and then out into the grey murkiness of the North Sea bound for their German targets in broad daylight, at first with no vestige of fighter protection, their only answer to the Luftwaffe, here fighting a home game with all its advantages, the gunners in their turrets – especially the heroic 'tail-end Charlie', since most attacks came from that quarter and the fighters' tactic was to try and eliminate the occupant of that glass showcase. In the late afternoon anxious eyes would scour the north eastern sky – then the dreadful counting, quite often suddenly petering out into silence, as disbelieving looks were exchanged in the Control Tower. Then a straggler or two would be spotted limping in, to literally collapse on its home runway – as the 'meat wagon' with its red crosses rushed out to retrieve what it could.

Nobody could doubt the personal bravery and persistent dedication to their task of these men; despite what was construed by British military norms as a more lax regime of discipline. The answer was probably a difference in outlook and temperament: the Americans attached less importance to the formalities of Service life, but certainly no less to its ultimate purpose. And they played hard, too. The two vital commodities that all the well-planned bases could not provide were girls and liquor. But with their outgoing and casually carefree approach to life – in a way that would be unimaginable in the indigeonous population, if *they'd* found themselves in a strange environment thousands of miles from home! – they soon solved those two problems: the local pubs were taken over by friendly, talkative invaders who readily introduced themselves, thoroughly educated the locals about whatever locality in the States they hailed from – and drank the place dry; and if the other wartime problem of glass shortages arose, they soon exchanged gum for jam jars and carried on. Not only were they extremely generous and considerate but they also had a remarkable facility for making allowances for those who did criticise them – and armed with these potent attributes they soon had little trouble in resolving the second problem. By good fortune, Norfolk and Suffolk, apart from being geographically right for bombing the Third Reich, were ideal for the great agricultural putsch

Groundcrewmen of the US Eighth Air Force change propellers of a twin-engined Lightning, one of the fighters that was introduced to provide cover for the daylight raids; at a base in Norfolk.

A dance at a Land Army Camp in Norfolk – the girls dance with their US Air Force guests.

– and another invasion was that of the Land Army Girls, also mostly bivouaced in uni-sex premises far from home. With – "Come on, Babe, how about you stepping out with me, huh? Gee! You *do* look great!" the first intimation a girl got of their presence, reciprocity was virtually impossible to refuse and soon they were well inducted into the jazz and jitterbug craze that was so pervasive of the times. An awful lot of genuine companionship was shared and the last hours of some of these men were at least enjoyable ones.

In January 1943 the US Eighth Air Force had nearly 600 bombers in constant operation, mostly out of the two counties; and in May 1944 the first of the 1000 bomber raids left the loamy flat landscape on their war-shortening work. Today, where turkeys parade the precincts of the "Mighty Eighth's" flyers and their long vanished hardware, to stand in a quiet spot and listen, it's possible for the imagination to hear the roar of engines, the screech of rubber on concrete, the voices and the music; and to feel the triumph and the tragedy of war.

BERNARD MATTHEWS P.L.C.

They all know the brass-word

They pass the word along the line:
'Brasso's the stuff to give the shine'

THEY ALL KNOW THE BRASS-WORD

A typical advertisement of Reckitt & Colman's for 'Brasso' during the war years.

Churchill tank crew relax, Holland 1945.

Winston Churchill leaves Headquarters, Maastricht, for the front.

VICKERS P.L.C.

THE SWORDFISH FLYS OVER CONVOY

I.W.M.

The Fairey Swordfish II torpedo spotter and reconnaissance aircraft, known affectionately as string bags, was invaluable to the convoys. There cannot ever have been a much harder test of courage - to be stationed on deck with the solitary inefficient gun and to see nothing to shoot at, but to see columns of smoke after a ship was torpedoed, or to sweat in the strokehold hearing nothing but the explosions. A welcoming sight of a Swordfish overhead, gave some comfort to the men of the convoy.

SWORDFISH II

Powered by Bristol Pegasus 30 engine; armament of 303. Vickers machine gun, an 18" torpedo, or depth charges had a range of 750 miles.

SHIPS CAT

Many Cats sailed with their ships during the war, a lot lost many of their nine lives, but many also had a cosy life as seen in this picture.

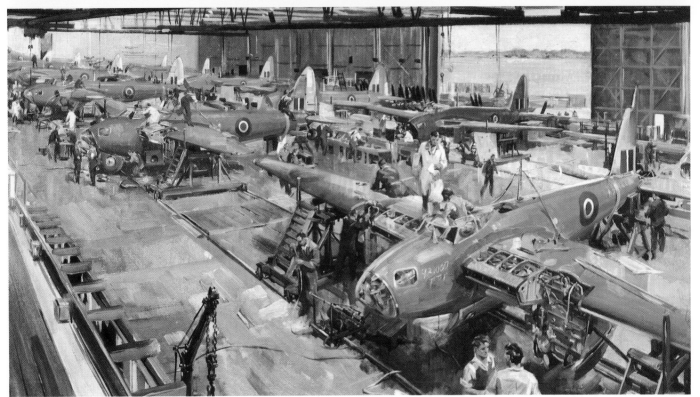

The remarkable high performance De Havilland Mosquito, versatile in many specialised roles, was based on a wooden airframe built by the furniture factories of High Wycombe, Buckinghamshire.

TERENCE CUNEO, BLAZE FINE ART

WING COMMANDER LEONARD CHESHIRE DROPPING TARGET INDICATOR FLARES ON THE GESTAPO HEADQUARTERS IN MUNICH – 24th APRIL 1944

By April 1944, Bomber Command had at its disposal many squadrons of Lancaster, Stirling and Halifax heavy bombers. Main Force attacks were usually spearheaded by the Pathfinder Force whose task it was to find the target and mark the aiming point with long-burning, brightly coloured flares known as Target Indicators.

No. 5 Group of Bomber Command had developed a very accurate system of low level visual marking. It was first used in March 1944 by No. 617 Squadron against targets in occupied countries where accuracy was of prime importance in reducing casualties amongst the friendly civilian population.

On 24 April 1944, whilst the main weight of Bomber Command was directed against Karlsruhe, No. 5 Group attacked the railway marshalling yards at Munich. The Marker Force consisted of four Mosquitoes led by Wing Commander Cheshire. The City was very heavily defended and he came under intense anti-aircraft fire as he dived from 12,000 to 700 feet to find and mark

the aiming point. After dropping his Target Indicator Flares, Cheshire continued to fly over the City at a height of only 1,000 feet directing the attack; his aircraft was hit several times and he was frequently blinded by searchlights. Amongst the buildings damaged during the attack was the Gestapo Headquarters in the City.

Later in 1944, having been engaged on bomber operations almost continuously since 1939, Cheshire was awarded the Victoria Cross in recognition of his outstanding gallantry and leadership. He was the official British Observer at the dropping of the atomic bomb on Nagasaki. After the war, he left the Royal Air Force and has since devoted his life to helping physically and mentally handicapped adults and children and is known throughout the world as the Founder of the Cheshire Homes.

Leonard Cheshire died on 31st of July 1992.

INTELLIGENCE CORPS. 'OPERATION BODYLINE'

The Army Photographic Interpretation Section became B Section of the newly formed Central Interpretation Unit in October 1940 and was charged with the study of German ground defences and artillery sites in occupied Europe.

In 1943 the Section was ordered to watch especially for new design, long-range artillery likely to be used to bombard England. It was suspected that rocket research was going on at Peenemunde and that a new weapon, capable of being fired from a long tube, was being developed. Although no trace of such a system could be found, the photographic interpreters (PIs) did locate a number of unusual construction sites in the Pas de Calais area. Some 70 locations were plotted, each having two blockhouses, a curving 'ski-type' blast wall and a ramp. The PIs analysis was put to the Air Ministry but the suggestion that the sites could be used to launch some new type of aircraft was dismissed. However, on 25th November 1943, on a test ramp at Peenemunde, the first sighting was made of a 'flying bomb' – the V1. It was obvious that the construction sites discovered by B Section were designed to launch this deadly weapon. The Air Ministry was notified at once and the Cabinet was briefed. As a result, 'Operation Bodyline' was initiated and a special section set up to intensify the search for V1 sites. Within ten days, 96 sites had been identified and Bomber Command was ordered to destroy them; before the end of the year,

92 had been eliminated. Then, in April 1944, B Section identified the first of a series of new, modified sites in Northern France. Although virtually all interpretation resources were now concentrated on D Day preparations, the Section still managed to locate 67 new flying bomb sites and on 1 June the Air Ministry was warned that they were operational. 34 hours later the first V1 landed on London. Bomber Command made further strikes but the needs of the Normandy invasion precluded complete destruction of all the new sites and 45 of them were still operational in mid-June. By the end of June some 2,000 V1s had been launched against London and the South-east of England.

B section's belief that the actual missiles were not kept at the launching sites but in the Neucourt caves, in the Some area, was proved correct when, in July, following movement in that region, a total of 106 V1s were launched. B Section requested a Bomber Command raid on Neucourt. The raid was successful and thereafter no V1s were launched from the Somme area.

Cuneo's painting shows members of B Section at Medmenham, Bucks, plotting V1 sites in December 1943. The contribution this small unit, less than 30 all ranks, made to the destruction of the flying bomb sites was, by any measure, outstanding.

A Gloster Meteor, the RAF's first jet which entered service in July 1944, tips a V1 flying-bomb into a violent 'wingover', causing it to crash in open country - the only alternative action when the Meteor's guns jammed.

DOG SEARCHES FOR V-1 BOMB VICTIMS
A dog working with a civil defence volunteer to discover victims after a V-1 bomb raid.

One of the most moving pictures of the war on the Home Front. Following a V-1 attack, a woman rescue worker lifts a distraught child from the ruins of a wrecked building in Buckingham Gate, Victoria 23 June, 1944. The 'doodlebug' attacks were not confined to the south-east. By firing V-1s from converted bombers, the Germans spread the attacks over a wider geographical area. For example, 27 people in Oldham were killed by a V-1 on Christman Eve, 1944.

Steam jets being used to clear ice on board HMS Sylla.

Collision – damage to the bows of the battleship HMS King George V.

HMS Honeysuckle in the Russian port of Murmansk.

CONVOYS TO RUSSIA

The convoys on the Arctic route, to keep the Russian war effort supplied, were commonly recognised as the most hazardous of all, passing close to occupied Norway, with its German submarine and aircraft bases, as well as fjord anchorages for warships. It was not only British seamen who endured this terrible route, there were Danes, Norwegians and Americans. It was a ten-day voyage to the Russian ports, such as Murmansk, and of the 811 merchant ships that attempted this massive support for Russia, in forty convoys, ninety-two were sunk; that was a one-in-nine chance of disaster amidst freezing seas; after which an unladen return voyage repeated the odds. In the Arctic summer the enemy had twenty-four hours of daylight in which to attack, the eternal vigilance exhausting many crews; while in winter though the perpetual darkness gave more protection, the ferocity of the elements more than compensated: mountainous seas, freezing fog, and snow and ice on the rigging, tophamper and guns was atrocious and had to be removed for stability and to be ready for action at any time. Close station had of necessity to be kept and extreme vigilance was called-for to avoid collision, as another hazard – with the ever-present knowledge that survival was only a matter of a few minutes in the icy water.

TERENCE CUNEO

THE TIDE TURNS IN BURMAH – KHOHIMA, 1944

After the Japanese had entered the War in December 1941, their well-organised armies, not only trained to high proficiency in modern fighting skills and weapons, but also imbued with a fanatical bravery that eschewed any notion of surrender, as well as superb junglecraft; soon made short work of the materially and psychologically ill-equipped defences of the British possessions.

Forced back onto the borders of India, with all Malaysia and Burma occupied, the task of recreating, in both morale and readiness, a new Fourteenth Army of British and Indian divisions, fell to General Slim. After the initial, and first time ever defeat of a Japanese force down the Arakan coast, in March 1944 he had to face their main attack against Imphal, a vast supply dump from which the road ran via Khohima to the railhead some 150 miles north at Dimaphur, the jugular of communications with India. Concentrating his forces on the Imphal plain they were soon locked in battle, but with typical Japanese strategy a further force bypassed this action and thrust for the main objective of Dimaphur – stopping off to tackle the purely guard garrison of the 4th Royal West Kents and Assam Regiment at Khohima. This small force was to take on 15,000 crack Japanese troops and so disrupt their overall strategy that Dimaphur and the way to India were saved; it was the turning point in the hitherto triumphant Asian progress of the Japanese Imperial Army. At such close quarters was this bloody engagement fought, that the opposing lines were only separated by the District Commissioners tennis court. After three months of intense struggle, much of it in monsoon downpours, Khohima and Imphal being supplied and re-inforced by air, the ceaseless ferocious assaults slackened; their supplies totally exhausted, the starving Japanese troops were by then eating grass. On the 8th July they fell back on Mandalay – a testimony to their terrible determination the 50,000 dead to only a handful of prisoners. The Fourteenth Army suffered 17,000 casualties.

Slim was now poised to start the long process, into 1945, of rolling back the Japanese occupation and reversing the humiliation to British prestige, starting with the reconquest of Burma which coincidentally was completed on the very day of the German surrender, the 5th May. But the plans for retaking Malaysia were suddenly obsolescent when the Japanese Empire surrendered in August, heralding mankind's entry into the nuclear age and the challenges of the second half of the twentieth century – but on a patch of Burmah, where the very English game of tennis would be played no more, a simple plinth bears the words:

'When you go home tell them of us and say for your
tomorrow we gave our today.'

DAVID BROWN   SIR ALEXANDER GIBB & PARTNERS LTD

START OF A TEN MILE BRIDGE - MULBERRY HARBOUR
One of the massive caisson constructions that were required for the Mulberry
Harbours. This great civil engineering project was undertaken by ten consulting
engineering companies and over twenty different contractors, at locations all over
the south and west of England. Between August 1943 and D-day, six miles of rein-
forced concrete caissons were formed, with ten miles of floating bridging supported by hundreds of concrete and steel pontoons and 23 special pierheads.

LAING'S CHARITABLE TRUST

June 1944 – rows of landing craft along Southampton's new docks – ready for 'D Day'.

WORLD WAR II EFFORT AT SOUTHAMPTON

Within a few years of their completion, the new docks at Southampton took on a completely new role. The days before the outbreak of the Second World War saw a build-up of troops and equipment in the docks. The passenger liners were moved to less vulnerable bases, many of them converted to armed merchant cruisers or troopships. With the collapse of France, the port's role as a supply bridge-head for the British Expeditionary Force was enhanced.

Early in 1943, preparations began for the invasion of France. Much of the famous 'Mulberry Harbour', to be floated across the Channel, was constructed in the dock area.

Before 'D-Day', troops and equipment were loaded on to landing craft which left for anchorages in Southampton Water prior to the Channel crossing.

During the war years, there were 69 air-raids affecting the docks, resulting in 23 transit sheds or warehouses being destroyed; there were 800 casualties in Southampton. Over 4.3 million troops passed through the port and 3.9 million tons of stores and equipment were handled.

(ABP wishes to thank Mr Bert Moody and Waterfront Publications.)

A section of the Mulberry Harbour at Southampton as pictured in the build-up to 'D Day'.

Terence Cuneo, Royal Artillery Collection

BATTLE OF MONTE CASSINO

Following the surrender on the 12th May 1943 of a quarter of a million Axis prisoners to the Eighth Army at Cap Bon in North Africa, this triumph was logically followed up by the Army (with the U.S. Seventh Army) landing in Sicily and after five weeks of heavy fighting, in Italy itself. On the 8th September, after Mussolini's resignation, Italy capitulated and the next day the Allies landed at Salerno, where their bridgehead was besieged as it soon became obvious that German determination to resist was unabated.

By the 1st October, Naples had been taken. Now it became clear that Field Marshal Kesselring, the German commander, was determined to exact a heavy price from the Eighth Army for any further progress up Italy towards Rome, assisted by ideal defensive terrain: broken mountainous country severed by a series of rivers, such as the Volturno and Rapido, swollen now by some atrocious weather. Behind these natural defences, through which the Army had to fight for every mile, lay the German main position, the Gustav Line, its epicentre the massive Monastery of Monte Cassino atop its mountain dominating Route 6, up the Liri Valley to Rome. An attempt to subvert the position by landing at Anzio in its rear collapsed when the Allied force failed to break out of a small foothold; and meanwhile Montgomery returned home for the invasion of North West Europe preparations, being succeeded by General Leese.

There now commenced one of the most epic contests of the war, involving three bitter and bloody months. Despite perpetual artillery bombardment, by over 600 heavy guns, reminiscent of the previous war's obliteration philosophy, and all that the Allied air forces could do to it, the position remained impregnable, shrugging off, at dauntingly heavy cost to the attackers, assaults from British, New Zealand, Indian and Polish units. It was only when Alexander managed, at last, to bypass the position by achieving a breakthrough where the Gustav Line approached the western Italian coast, using thirteen divisions in the process, that Monte Cassino finally gave in to the Eighth Army.

It fell to the Americans to enter Rome on the 4th June 1944 and two days later the Normandy beaches were stormed successfully and the Second Front was at last a reality; to many it seemed the end of fighting in both Italy and France was just a matter of time – just how long, and difficult, that time was to be, was not that obvious.

D-DAY

After more than two year's planning and 24 hours postponement the intensively defended beaches of Normandy were stormed in the early hours of 6th June 1944 by the British Second Army under General Dempsey with the U.S. First Army; Field Marshal Montgomery being in overall command. British XXX Corps landed on 'Gold' beach near Aromanches, to its left the 3rd Canadian Division and beyond them, the 3rd British Division of 1 Corps landed on 'Juno' and 'Sword' beaches, both west of the Orne River, to the east of which, high ground and heavy coastal artillery posed a threat to the landing area, which was removed by an audacious parachute and glider assault by 6th Airborne Division; after which the specialised tanks of 79th Armoured Division led the infantry ashore, despite the web of obstacles. By nightfall all objectives had been achieved – except Caen, where a German armoured division blocked 3rd Division's access to the town.

Unable to bypass this strong point, Montgomery decided to use it as a lure to attract German armoured strength to repel his all out attacks on the town, which was at the eastern end of the bridgehead, thus leaving the Americans less opposition to breakthrough at the western perimeter. For days the situation was stalemated, threatening the whole Allied strategy, but fortunately Caen was captured on the 8th July and a heavy offensive drive through the narrow sunken lanes, bordered by hedges, that were the infantry's highly dangerous fighting ground, fanned out into the interior. By the end of that month, the British and Canadians had attracted six strong panzer divisions, assisting the Americans to break through their opposition of only two and drive south and east into comparatively open country.

This mobility enabled a flanking movement to pocket-off almost all the German formations that had been deployed in the Normandy salient, around the town of Falaise, birthplace of another successful cross-Channel invader, William the Conqueror; the armour being destroyed by rocket-firing fighter aircraft, who by now enjoyed almost complete command of the coastal skies, and the infantry taken prisoner; setting the seal on any doubts about Europe's forthcoming liberation.

DAY AND NIGHT - NORMANDY   *I.W.M.*

Laundary and gardening go on in an English front line town, while streams of American men and material roll down the streets on their way over to France. Day and night, the town throbs with the sound of armoured vehicles moving up to reinforce Allied troops advancing inland in France against the Germans.

I.W.M.

H.M.S Rodney adds her weight of shells to the Navy's pounding of enemy positions along the Caen Coast.

GKN DEFENCE

JOHNNIE JOHNSON'S CANADIAN WING

One of the greatest exponents of the Spitfire was James Edgar Johnson, known within the RAF as "Johnnie" Johnson. After originally joining the TA, he transferred to the RAF and joined Nos. 19 and 616 Squadrons during 1940. An old shoulder injury asserted itself and Johnson had to go into hospital for surgery to correct it, and he did not rejoin No. 616 Squadron until December 1940.

During the fighter sweeps over the Continent during the summer of 1941, No. 616 Squadron was in Douglas Bader's Tangmere Wing, and Johnson often flew in Bader's section as his "Number Two".

Johnson shot down several German aircraft during 1941, and in the summer of the following year he was promoted to command No. 610 Squadron.

In February 1943, he was promoted again, this time to Wing Commander to lead the Canadian Wing at Kenley. In September of that year, with his score at 25, he was rested from operations and occupied a staff post.

In March 1944, he went back to operations, again as a Wing Leader with another Royal Canadian Air Force Wing, composed of Nos. 441, 442 and 443 Squadrons, where he had further successes.

This painting shows him leading his section from the Wing over the Normandy beaches on D-Day.

His Spitfire carries his initials JE-J (a Wing Commander's privilege), and all aircraft are marked with the special "D-Day stripes" in black and white. These markings were decreed by the Allied air commanders to avoid the shooting down of friendly aircraft by our own forces. They were carried by all aircraft except heavy bombers, both British and American, and were applied as a result of secret orders issued the evening before D-Day. No Allied aircraft except heavy bombers were allowed to fly without them.

Johnson led his squadrons in action right up to VE-Day, which found him in Denmark. Here he arranged a victory air show which was attended by Her Majesty the Queen of Denmark.

Johnson stayed in the Royal Air Force after the war, retiring in 1965 with the rank of Air Vice Marshal.

Left: Wing Commander Johnnie Johnson with his dog, Sally, and his Spitfire in the background; France 1944.

GLIDERS AT CAEN – 1944
Gliders with their D-Day markings landing at Caen.

FRANK WOOTON GAv.A

FLYING OVER NORMANDY
Spitfires of No 312 (Czech) Squadron fly over troops and armour, advancing to the front.

RONALD WONG GAv.A

Action of the Right Flank, 3rd Bn Scots Guards during the advance from Caumont to Les Loges, Normandy, 30 July 1944.   *TERENCE CUNEO*

SCOTS GUARDS IN THE BOCAGE

A month after D-Day, during which Field Marshal Montgomery's strategy of hammering away at the fortified town of Caen with the Second Army had concentrated German strength against the east of the Normandy bridgehead, on the 8th of July 1944 that town was taken. By then, while the British and Canadians faced six German panzer divisions, the Americans were opposed by only two and on the 25th they burst through the weakened enemy defences, driving south and then east. It was much more favourable than the situation which they'd met when they first tried to capture the communications centre of Saint Lo at the base of the Contentin Peninsula, an isthmus lying between the Normandy beaches and the Gulf of St Malo. It had involved fighting in the jungle-like area of the Bocage; the Commander of the U.S. 7th Corps (which ultimately captured Cherbourg, only to find it severely damaged and mined) General Collins had experienced these conditions before, in the jungles of Gualdalcanal where he'd previously served. His solution was to devise a form of giant hedge-cutter with which to deal with the undergrowth – but that did not solve the other problem of very broken terrain with exceptionally steep natural obstacles which were soon proving too much for his Sherman tanks either to climb or bypass. With the German defenders entrenched and hidden behind these features, the Americans suffered heavy casualties, only just able to reach Saint Lo, where they were totally halted on the 16th of July. On the same day, the British 5th Corps, under General O'Connor, began an advance southwards, to the east of Caen.

To the astonishment of not only the Americans, but more importantly the Germans, the 3rd Bn Scots Guards advanced rapidly through the Bocage – owing to their length and also the weight of their tracks, their Churchill Tanks proved that they were the only ones capable of surmounting the exceptionally high banks without turning over backwards. The action depicted is the right flank of the 3rd Bn, during the advance from Caumont to Les Loges, on the 30th of July – the commander of 'Lochinvar' survived to become Bishop of St Albans and later Archbishop of Canterbury. At the time, he was Lieutenant Robert Runcie, in the process of winning his Military Cross.

ROBERT FLEMING HOLDINGS

THE ROYAL SCOTS WAR

The 1st Battalion The Royal Scots was part of the British Expeditionary Force sent to France in September 1939. When the Allies failed to hold the German attack through Belgium in May 1940, the Battalion was part of the force holding the perimeter during the evacuation from Dunkirk. Few survived and the Battalion had to be reformed in UK. In 1942, it was sent to India to help stem the Japanese advance. In January 1943, they were involved in the first counter offensive in the Arakan which unfortunately failed. But, in 1944, the Battalion was deployed as part of 2nd Infantry Division to relieve Kohima and, on the successful conclusion of that campaign, took part in the advance to Mandalay and the defeat of the Japanese forces in Burma.

After the successful Allied landings in Normandy Montgomery's overall plan was to force the Germans to deploy their reserves and concentrate their strength against the British and Canadians at the East end of the Bridgehead. This would allow the Americans, in the West to break-out against relatively weak opposition. This involved some very heavy fighting especially around Caen.

The Normandy countryside afforded every advantage to a defender with small fields bounded by thick set hedges growing above stout banks and intersected by sunken lanes. Attacking through it became a series of small infantry battles with tanks in support after the enemy anti tank guns had been destroyed. During one such battle for the villages of Gavrus and Bougy, Brigadier Clark who was commanding a Tank Brigade, described the action of the 8th Battalion The Royal Scots as follows: "It was sticky - for the Boche was on three sides. This area was one of the unsafest places I know of at that time. The capture of Gavrus and Bougy was a classical example of tank and infantry cooperation.

NORMANDY 1944

THE ROYAL SCOTS (The Royal Regiment)

ROBIN SALVESEN

ALAN FEARNLEY, The Military Gallery, Bath

ARNHEM – A BRIDGE TOO FAR

After Normandy, the Allies began their inexorable and at times rapid advance across France, Paris having been spared by the Germans as a 'free' city. With Five Star General Dwight Eisenhower in overall command, the 21st Army Group, with the First Canadian Army, formed the left, northern, flank where, the Guards Armoured Division having entered Brussels on the 3rd September, Montgomery now believed all efforts ought to be concentrated to overcome the stiffening German resistance on the borders of Holland and Germany itself, and a push made to take the country's industrial heartland, the Ruhr, and thence straight on to Berlin. Considerable disagreement developed with the Americans, who favoured their own three armies making up a southern front, between the Ardennes and Switzerland, and all forces advancing in one simultaneous line on the German border.

Perhaps partly to demonstrate his strategy's efficacy, Montgomery launched 'Market Garden', an operation which was to cut a corridor with XXX Corps straight across 60 miles of country, seizing bridges that crossed the Maas, the Waal – and, at Arnhem, the Rhine; putting the Allied advance on the Dutch coast, at the then existing Zuider Zee, across the psychological barrier that the Rhine represented and indeed, poised on the threshold of the Ruhr.

The initial bridges being taken by two U.S. Airborne divisions, part of the U.S. First Army placed in Montgomery's sector as Eisenhower's compromise, things began to go badly wrong: in deteriorating weather the 1st Airborne Division under Major General Urquhart destined for a drop at Arnhem's bridge, landed some distance away, almost on top of two crack S.S. Panzer Divisions, only Lt. Col. Frost's 2nd Parachute Battalion managing to reach the bridge and dig in, resisting with superb gallantry and resourcefulness the understandably very determined German efforts to dislodge them. While the remaining eight battalions battled in a shrinking perimeter on the outskirts of the town, the weather closed and stopped further airborne operations; and meanwhile the column coming overland, spearheaded by the Guards Armoured Brigade, were reaping the fruits of poor intelligence as they found their progress restricted to a road, with impassable boggy land either side, that allowed only a one-tank front; in the face of strong anti-armour defences. By the 22nd September the Guards had ground to a halt only five miles from Arnhem, learning that Frost's gallant band on the bridge had succumbed hours before; and on the 24th Urquhart signalled that, after the 25th, his force would suffer the same fate: he was ordered to withdraw the 2,000 survivors of his original 10,000 to safety across the Rhine, so ending 'Market Garden' – Montgomery's bid to conclude the War in 1944.

AIR SEA RESCUE

ASR saved many thousands of lives during the war. There were units right round the coasts of the British Isles and they operated in the North Sea, the Channel and Western approaches. There were famous units operating out of Malta and elsewhere in the Mediterranean, and indeed worldwide.

Throughout their operations the ASR has brought back many survivors. Indeed the ASR coined the phrase, "The sea shall not have them".

Sometimes, especially in the wintertime, it was pretty dicey, going out in the night time in rough seas. The ASR launches were more like submarines than surface ships. However, they *always* went, come Hell or High Water. It was often High Water and sometimes a bit of Hell, but that was the lot of most services anyway. The ASR had a marvellous bunch of seagoing crews – businessmen, tycoons, errand boys, every possible mixture. On the big boats there was a crew of 11. Speeds were quite fast, the fastest (107) clocked 38/40 knots, generally speeds reached were between 25 and 37 knots. One of the better known boats was the Scott-Paine Whaleback, a streamliner which used to bash its way through the tops of waves and bounce from one to the next in gay abandon.

In the summertime the crews would rev up and use top speed in more moderate seas and go off on a job looking for a tiny speck (or specks) of a yellow dinghy containing an ever hopeful pilot or crew member – often wondering how long it would take finding him.

Many of these craft were powered by three Perkins S6 marine engines. Today there are few better examples of partnership, than Perkins association with GKN, which helped to produce the Warrior armoured fighting vehicle for the British Army. This internationally acclaimed equipment was combat tested to great effect during the Gulf War.

PERKINS GROUP LIMITED

JOHN HAMILTON I.W.M.

L.A. BRIDGE C.F.V.A.

COASTAL FORCES OPERATONS IN THE MIDDLE EAST: MTBs IN ACTION.

The few available MTB's and ML's commenced operations in North Africa against the Germans. At great risks and with heavy losses these small vessels ranged along the North African coast attacking German supply routes. The beleaguered garrison of Tobruk was supplied by MTB's and ML's operating from Egyptian bases.

Later, after the surrender of Italy, bases were established on the Italian main-land including Bari, Brindisi, etc. Operations included Salerno and Anzio Landings and dangerous patrols in the Straits of Messina.

In the Adriatic, Coastal Vessel's were given the task of assisting Tito and his partisans by running guns and supplies. Eventually, a base was established at Komiza on the Yugoslav Island of Vis. Patrols were always dangerous, the Adriatic was heavily mined and patrolled by the Germans, main targets were supply vessels and torpedo and gun action were the order of the day and night, losses were heavy on both sides.

The Flotillas consisted of the large, heavily armed "D" Class MTBs, known as the "Dogs", British designed 70' MTBs built in the USA and many Motor Launches, maids of all work which carried Army/Partisan raiding parties and did mine-sweeping. Crew's varied from 12 to 30 with young officers and younger crew members. Many of the boats were either damaged or sunk by mines in the shallow waters; a problem which was negligible in UK waters.

Tito outside his HQ with his dog called 'Tiger'

THE BRAVE DANES – AND THEIR SHIPS

Over 6,000 Danish seamen chose to remain with their ships in the "foreign" fleet during the war. They sailed on all the seas with every kind of cargo and, for the majority, it was a stormy and nerve-wracking period, for many ending in death. On the 24 wrecked Maersk ships alone, nearly 100 Danes perished and many others were marked for life.

A brass band welcome, for a brave ship and crew, as it enters Malta.

THE MAERSK COMPANY LIMITED

TERENCE CUNEO

THE CROSSING OF THE RHINE

After the failure of Operation 'Market Garden' to end the war in 1944, that winter the Germans launched an unexpected and daring offensive against a weak American sector in the Ardennes, aimed at recapturing Antwerp, whose port the Allies had taken intact (when British tanks clandestinely tricked their way through its defences, guided by the Belgian Resistance) but which had only just become available for use, after an enemy denial force had finally been removed from Walcheren, where they'd controlled the port's approaches via the River Scheldt. The German initiative was finally stopped in the Battle of the Bulge, during which Eisenhower had placed Montgomery in command of all U.S. formations involved on the northern flank of the salient.

In early January 1945 the 21st Army Group were locked in heavy fighting as the First Canadian Army (nine of whose thirteen divisions were British) slogged southwestwards through mud and rain against fierce opposition in the Reichswald Forest to clear the west bank of the Rhine, till it linked up with the Americans to the west of the Wesel.

On the night of the 23rd-25th March, under cover of an immense bombardment, a crossing of the Rhine was forced. As an observer watching the 44th Bn The Royal Tank Regiment, 4th Armoured Brigade, commented later: "It is quite unbelievable that these primitive toy-like canvas boats could be successful in floating Sherman Tanks across a river. But they were. A piece of invention that beggars belief."

The tanks rapidly joined up with the 6th Airborne Division, which had been dropped to the east of the river to facilitate the quick build-up of a bridgehead. By the end of March the Allies had surrounded the Ruhr, the industrial heartland that had been a primary objective to end Germany's war effort, (a

bonus being when they later found that a railway bridge at Remagen, though completely mined for destruction, had not in fact been blown – the only bridge over the Rhine the Germans had failed to destroy). Montgomery was all set to head straight for Berlin, but to his astonishment Eisenhower now decided to make the main effort towards Dresden with the U.S. armies, leaving the Russians to take Berlin, with not only the psychological advantage but all that was implied and did in fact occur in postwar Europe, beginning with the need for the Berlin Airlift, so soon afterwards. The 21st Army Group was left to protect the American northern flank by an advance on Bremen and Hamburg.

XXX Corps still met some fanatical resistance but the Third Reich was on the point of collapse (trying to defend the west bank of the Rhine, in deference to Hitler's orders, and the execution squads of the SS, had cost a quarter of a million of the most effective still remaining German troops as casualties or prisoners).

As the spring of 1945 got under way, the 2nd of May was to be a date that in the gloom of that spring five years earlier could only be imagined: the bomb devastated city of Hamburg fell to the 7th Armoured Division, ending the last lap of its long journey from the Western Desert which had begun in 1940, the 11th Armoured, 6th Airborne and the 5th Division reached Lübeck and the Baltic coast and, far away south across the Alps, the Eighth Army rolled into Venice and Trieste to complete its saga of victory since Alamein, as the Germans in Italy formally capitulated.

On the 4th of May all German forces in Holland and northwest Europe surrendered to Montgomery in a tent on Lüneburg Heath, hostilities actually ceasing at 8.00 am on the 5th of May – World War II in Europe was over.

Ronald Wong G Av. A.

Low flying Lancasters dropping food parcels over Holland 1945.

I.W.M.

The Feast of St Nicholas, a party for the Dutch children 1945.

WESTMINSTER DREDGING Co. Ltd.

German E-boats berthed at the Dock basin in May 1945.

The Port of Felixstowe from the air, with the North Sea at bottom right, Trinity Container Terminal at top left and the original Dock basin in the centre.

STONE FRIGATE SAILS INTO ACTION

FELIXSTOWE Dock basin in wartime was the "stone frigate" HMS Beehive, a home for the Royal Navy's smallest surface attack units. In peacetime the Dock basin became the nucleus of the modern Port of Felixstowe, which attracts the world's largest containerships and handles more containers than its main British rivals put together. The transition began with the formal surrender at Felixstowe of the enemy Schnellboote (or E-boat) fleet on May 13, 1945. Rear Admiral Karl Bruening arrived with two of these sleek grey craft that crossed the North Sea at speeds of up to 32 knots. He brought charts of minefields that had to be swept before international commerce could resume. Motor torpedo boats from Felixstowe helped to resist the invasion of the Netherlands in 1940 and shot down at least one German aircraft. They brought back Dutch refugees, then saw action off Zeebrugge and Dunkirk and took part in the Dunkirk evacuation. Felixstowe-based MTBs and motor gunboats went out to tackle German convoys and marauding E-boats, torpedoing vessels and

actually capturing an E-boat, which sank before it could be towed back to the Dock. Lieutenant-Commander Ian Trelawny, one of the Beehive heroes, became the port executive who pioneered UK containerisation at Felixstowe. History was also made at the place where this container concept began: by the Army in 1667, when the garrison of Landguard Fort beat off 2,000 Dutch marines in the last true invasion of England, and by the Royal Air Force in the development of high-speed seaplanes. They included Supermarine floatplanes that won the international Schneider Trophy for this country in 1927, 1929 and 1931 – a hat trick that secured the trophy for all time.

The achievement led to the Rolls-Royce Merlin engine powering the Supermarine Spitfire, which fought so well in the Battle of Britain. The Port of Felixstowe has always worked with this spirit while setting new standards for the transport industry.

THE PORT OF FELIXSTOWE

American Ambulance Girls in London - the terrier, 'Brix', was rescued from a house bombed in Brixton; and below: dog models steel helmet and gas mask case.

1,486,157,464 SERVICE BISCUITS

In November 1945 that month's issue of Spratt's famous magazine for dog-owners, *The Tailwagger*, was able to announce (in the jargon of the times) "It may now be revealed ..." why it had not always been possible during the war for readers' pets to have the Spratt's Biscuit Food that they had preferred.

"There was a huge demand from Government Departments and the Services for Biscuits. More and more Biscuits was the pressing need. Biscuits! More Biscuits! Spratt's (part of Spillers Foods) made White Biscuits; Brown Biscuits; Biscuits for the Army; Biscuits for Sailors; Biscuits to American recipes for U.S Troops; Special Biscuits to combat cold and exposure, for rafts and lifeboats; Biscuits for submarines; Emergency Biscuits for the civilian population in times of raids or disorganised conditions; Biscuits in special sealed tins and Biscuits for War Dogs in training or serving in "the field."

Though staffs were depleted with the Call Up, the Company's output was enormous. Enough Service Biscuits alone were made to stretch across the Atlantic Ocean more than twenty times. In the first period of greatest urgency their factories worked seven days a week continuously round the clock. Even later, when some relaxation was found to be imperative, the greater part of the vast bakeries still managed to run for 24 hours. Women responded to the challenge, undertaking tasks previously thought far too arduous for feminine hands. Despite their responsibilities in the direct war effort, they were able to maintain a limited flow of Spratt's famous Dog Foods for home consumption, and though these were 'austerity' products, they were still made to the best possible standard and with all the care and experience that had made famed that household name to generations of Britons.

HOME LEAVE
A welcome kiss and perhaps a bar or two of Cadbury's chocolate?

CADBURY SCHWEPPES Plc

Vera Lynn in a BBC studio. On the extreme left is the urbane figure of Alvar Lidell, doyen of announcers, who brought news both good and bad to the public in tones of patrician calm.

ENSA

ENSA was born in August 1939 and was the brainchild of Basil Dean, the theatrical producer and film magnate, who had been a pioneer of troop entertainment in the First World War. Dean was convinced that in the coming conflict servicemen would need and demand, professional entertainment. His plan was to organise his own army of artists, covering the whole range of the entertainment business, who would be prepared to go anywhere to entertain the men in the forces.

ENSA performed wonders both in Britain and overseas, often in the most gruelling and hazadous conditions, entertaining troops from North Aftrica to Burma. In the Spring of 1944 Vera Lynn toured the Arakan Front in Burma, and she still remembers the slap of the huge jungle insects dive-bombing her accompanist's piano keys as they homed in on the lights of her improvised stage.

ENSA had been quick into the field, but the early months of its life were dogged by a combination of muddle and acrimony which clung to it throughout the war. The quality of ENSA's shows was, to put it mildly, extemely variable. It was shows like these – immensely game but irredeemably fifth-rate – which earned Dean's organisation the nickname 'Every Night Something Awful'. However, Dean later modified his approach to the range of entertainment provided by ENSA. As the comedian Charlie Chester observed, at the beginning of the war the accent had been on 'tits and tinsel'. But with the call-up of older age-groups and the mixing of the classes in the services, the ENSA programme was expanded to include more 'highbrow' entertainment.

ENSA was disbanded in 1947. At its peak in the war it was mounting some 500 shows a week at home and abroad. Many of the stars of the future began their careers in an ENSA show. It attracted its fair share of criticism, from the 'blue' jokes of comics like Tommy Trinder to its erratic appearances in remote theatres of war. But the relief, laughter and occasional enlightenment it brought to civilians and servicemen during the war remain its true monument.

After fifty years Dame Vera Lynn is still lifting the hearts of men and women everywhere, who lived and fought throughout World War II. She has recently published a paperback of her life on the Home Front 'We'll Meet Again,' published by Sidgwick & Jackson, part of MACMILLAN PUBLISHERS.

Vera Lynn in her ENSA uniform, popularly known as 'Basil Dress', after the organisation's director Basil Dean.

MACMILLAN PUBLISHERS LTD

A LANCASTER WITH 100 OPERATIONS

This veteran Lancaster R5868 is shown here surrounded by air and ground crew of No. 467 Squadrom (RAAF) on the occasion of successfully concluding its 100th operation. The aircraft, carrying the unit codes PO-S, eventually went on to complete at least 137 sorties and is now preserved for posterity in the Royal Air Force Museum at Hendon.

It was customary for each successful sortie to be displayed on the fuselage near the pilot's cockpit, and this was usually done by the use of a small bomb symbol. The wording "No Enemy Plane Will Fly Over the Reich Territory" is taken from a speech made by Hermann Goering, the Chief of the German Air Force, just before the war, and emphasises in mocking fashion the sorties of the RAF over Germany.

Also shown on the aircraft are some of the decorations won by the crews which flew in "S-Sugar".

R5868 was originally "Q-Queenie" of No. 83 Squadron and flew its first sortie over enemy territory on the night of 8/9 July 1942 against Wilhelmshafen. After completing 79 sorties with No. 83 Squadron (the last against Milan on 12/13 August 1943) the aircraft was sent for a thorough over-haul, and was eventually re-issued to No. 467 Squadron in November 1943.

It next flew on opertions again on the night of 26/27 November 1943 when the target was Berlin, and completed its 100th operation against Bourg Leopold, Belgium, on 11/12 May 1944. Its last operation was on 23 April 1945, and for several years it stood at the main gate of RAF Scampton before being refurbished and put on display in the RAF Museum.

THE AUXILIARY TERRITORIAL SERVICE (ATS) – PRINCESS AND OTHER AUXILIARIES

In December 1941 women were conscripted into the Service and for essential work in industry. The strength of the ATS rose from 17,614 in August to a peak of 215,000 in June 1943. The initial 5 trades increased to 124.

The first party of ATS to serve outside the UK were sent to France in the spring of 1940 and were subsequently evacuated with the British Expeditionary Force. During the Second World War the ATS served in the Middle East, India, Washington, Ceylon, Palestine, Malaya, Austria, Eritrea, Algeria, Australia and Italy. Following the Normandy landings, a mixed Heavy Anti-Aircraft Regiment went to North West Europe to deal with the V1 and V2 bombs which were being launched from inside Germany.

In the spring of 1945, Her Royal Highness Princess Elizabeth joined the ATS, was commissioned as a Second Subaltern, and trained at No 1 Motor Transport Training Centre at Camberley.

The run-down of the ATS began in 1945 with the beginning of demobilisation, but a small and effcent service continued to function until the Women's Royal Army Corps, the WRAC, came into being in February 1949.

THE AIR TRANSPORT AUXILIARY

One of the lesser known organisations which contributed to victory during the Second World War was the Air Transport Auxiliary. This organisation was formed in September 1939 from civilians who already held flying licences. Its task was to deliver aircraft from the factories to the RAF.

Most of its personnel were those who had been employed in some capacity in the aviation industry, or those who held private pilot's licences, but were unable to serve in the RAF.

Originally, there were but 26 pilots, and by the end of the war there were at least 700 pilots on the strength of the ATA. Of these, about 100 were women.

The pilots were requried to be able to fly any type of aircraft, often with a minimum of tuition on each aircraft type. It was not unknown for pilots to handle several different types in one day. As an example, one pilot recorded in his logbook on one day delivery flights of a Stirling, a Sunderland, a Mosquito and a Liberator.

H.M. The Queen at H.M.T.E. DAUNTLESS

BRITISH AEROSPACE, HATFIELD : LONDON NEWS AGENCY

REUTER S.H.A.E.F
FLASH!!!
GERMANY SURRENDERED
UNCONDITIONALLY THIS
MORNING IT IS OFFICIALLY
ANNOUNCED
VC
- REUTER.

St Paul's in the afternoon sunlight among the bombed out ruins.

ST PAULS IN THE AFTERNOON SUNLIGHT

The last hours', at about 7.40pm, the Ministry of Information put the nation out of its misery, issuing a statement on the wireless. In a curious way it fell almost as flat as Neville Chamberlain's gloomy declaration of war on 3 September 1939. 'It is understood that, in accordance with arrangements between the three great powers, an official announcement will be broadcast by the Prime Minister at three O'clock tomorrow, Tuesday, will be treated as Victory-in-Europe Day and will be regarded as a holiday. His Majesty the King will broadcast to the people of the British Empire and Commonwealth tomorrow, Tuesday, at 9pm.' Thus, in the fussy, precise tones of a civil servant, was VE Day brought to the British public.

St Pauls from the air, showing devastation of the surrounding buildings.

I.W.M

CAZENOVE & CO.

VE-DAY PICCADILLY CIRCUS
Perched above a huge crowd in Piccadilly Circus, a small band of intrepid urban mountaineers celebrate on this statueless boarded-up plinth of Eros.

IWM

BUCKINGHAM PALACE ON VE-DAY
The moment of victory. The Royal Family and Churchill acknowledge the cheers of the crowd from the palace balcony.

WHITEHALL ON VE-DAY
Crowds stream past the Cenotaph in Whitehall on VE-Day while more intrepid souls view the proceedings from the roof of a Ministry building.

CHARTER plc

VICTORY CELEBRATIONS
Londoner's gather around Nelson's monument in Trafalgar Square during VE-Day celebrations.

IWM

ENTERPRISE OIL plc

Stamping names on the edges of medals.

Placing a Distinguished Flying Cross in its presentation case.

Hand engraving the recipient's name on the back of a George Cross.

Sewing the medal ribbon.

MEDALS FIT FOR HEROS

The Second World War generated an enormous requirement for medals and decorations, the Royal Mint having to enlist the assistance of Woolwich Arsenal in order to cope with the huge numbers needed at the end of the War. At the Mint, as these illustrations show, many of the ancillary processes were undertaken by women.

Filing the edges of Military Crosses.

The Royal Mint at Llantrisant today.

Since the War the Royal Mint has left London for the rolling green countryside of South Wales. The new mint at Llantrisant, near Cardiff, was opened by Her Majesty the Queen in December 1968 and now extends over a site of more than thirty acres.

ROYAL MINT

REUTERS – EYES AND EARS OF WAR

The reporting of wars has been the business of 'Reuters' for nearly a century and a half, since the Crimean War of 1854-56. Julius Reuter had founded his news agency in London in 1851. During the Second World War Reuters sent correspondents to all the main battlefronts. In September 1939 a Reuter man was chosen to be the first (and for several weeks the only) reporter with the British Expeditionary Force in France. Later in the war, Reuters was ahead with some notable stories, including first news of the German invasion of the Soviet Union in 1941. Harold King, chief correspondent in Moscow, covered the Russian recovery during 1943-44. He was first to tell of the Soviet breakthrough into the Balkans. 'During the night brave Cossak cavalrymen watered their horses in the Dneistr'. These words of praise meant that the Russians were into Romania. The Soviet censors might have delayed this story if it had been more plainly expressed, for it raised the question of whether Communism was to be for export. Censorship posed problems for Reuter correspondents on all the war fronts. They accepted that their stories might sometimes be blue pencilled; but otherwise Reuters insisted that what has passed for publication must be the truth, even if not the whole truth. It refused to circulate official propaganda or disiniformation. To make up numbers for D-day, Reuters recruited half a dozen young journalists from the United States, Canada and Ireland. But youngest of all the Allied correspondents on D-day was Doon Campbell, a twenty-four year old Scot. Despite being unfit for military service because of an arm disability, he landed for Reuters on 6 June 1944 with the first British seaborne assault. Like all good war reporters he neither minimised the dangers, nor took unnecessary risks. 'Much of my 24 hours have been spent flat on my face … I crouched for two hours in a ditch before realising I was a good 100 yards ahead of the forward troops.' On D-Day plus six (12 June) General Montgomery briefed nearly fifty correspondents at his headquarters, Campbell included. Monty announced that the Allies had won the battle of the beaches. Seaghan Maynes, an Irishman, slipped into Paris for Reuters in August 1944 ahead of the advancing troops, and got a message back, 'onpass Reuter', via the Resistance radio. A month later, Jack Smythe dropped by parachute for Reuters to cover the ill-fated Arnhem landings. He managed to send out the solitary press report. 'They fight individually as well as in platoons and companies. When the Second Army arrives and relieves this crowd, then may be told one of the epics of the war.' The army never did arrive, and smyth spent the rest of the European war as a prisoner. For the successful Rhine crossing in March 1945, Campbell landed by glider and Maynes parachuted down. 'The hunting horns of the paratroop commanders', reported Maynes, 'sounded the tally-ho to rally the units.' Hitler was personally receiving Reuter reports of the final advance on Berlin from west and east. He had always trusted Reuters, and what he read in his bunker contributed to his decision to commit suicide. A fortnight later news of the discovery by the Russians of what was thought to be his body was first reported by Reuters. It had done very well in its war reporting. The American General Patton congratulated Maynes: 'When I think of how much time you spent with the front-line troops I am at a loss to understand why more correspondents aren't dead'. On all fronts, five Reuters correspondents were killed during the Second World War. Twelve have been killed reporting conflicts since 1945. The risks are now greater than ever, because wars of liberation, civil wars or guerrilla campaigns are often fought without clearcut frontlines or rules of engagement. Today from all the world's troublespots Reuters transmits by satellite not only textual news, but also still photographs and television pictures. The technology and the immediacy are new; but the essentials of war reporting – the commitment to telling who is fighting who, where, how, why, and with what result – remain always the same.

JAPANESE 'KAMIKAZE' ATTACK ON A BRITISH AIRCRAFT CARRIER

It was early in 1945, just before the close of hostilities in Europe, that the British Pacific Fleet, chiefly comprising heavy aircraft carriers, joined up with the United States Pacific Fleet at Okinawa. The British Fleet was commanded by Admiral Sir Bruce Fraser, operating mainly from Sydney, Australia and from Guam. Commanding at sea was Vice-Admiral Sir Bernard Rawlings, in HMS *King George V*, and commanding the aircraft carrier squadron was Admiral Sir Philip Vian. This squadron comprised the carriers HMS *Indefatigable, Illustrious, Victorious* and *Indomitable*, each with about sixty aircraft on deck. During the Okinawa campaign, the role of this force, known as Task Force 57 and then Task Force 37, was to keep the Japanese air forces on Formosa from supporting their army in Okinawa.

The Japanese response to the attack on Okinawa was almost entirely a matter of Kamikaze suicide attacks from the air on the US and British Fleets. The Kamikazes made ten main attacks in April, May and June 1945, as well as many minor attacks. Over 1,400 suicide planes took part in the main attacks and they were accompanied by a similar number of bombers. They damaged the American Admiral Spruance's flagship *Indianapolis* so severely that he transferred his flag to the battleship *New Mexico*, which was in turn also hit by a Kamikaze on 12th May. On 6th/7th April 1945, some 355 Kamikazes and 341 other aircraft attacked the combined fleet. They sank three destroyers, an LST and two freighters, laden with ammunition. They also damaged seventeen other ships, some so severely that they were immediately scrapped at the end of the war.

Each of the British aircraft carriers was damaged quite badly by the Kamikazes. After about two weeks, *Illustrious*, still bearing the scars of an earlier campaign, was replaced by HMS *Formidable* and in June 1945, HMS *Implacable* joined the Pacific Fleet. In July and August, these ships joined the attacks on the Japanese mainland.

MICHAEL TURNER

Burma 1945. Battle of Kangaw – Royal Marine Commandos take cover as a Japanese maching-gun opens up from the bushes above their heads during the attack on hill 170.

Royal Marines of the British East Indies Fleet after landing at Port Swettenham, Penang, off the coast of Malaya in 1945. LSI Princess Beatrix.

As Nazi Germany re-armed in the mid-1930s, in defiance of the Versailles Treaty, war in Europe once again became a real possibility. Although outwardly in favour of appeasement, the British Government took no chances but initiated the far-sighted "Shadow Factory" scheme, under which factories would be built to "Shadow", and thus multiply the production facilities of, the nation's aircraft makers. For in a future war, supremacy in the air was already seen as vital.

Only a select few motor manufacturers with solid reputations were chosen to participate in this scheme, and among them was the Rover Company, then based in Coventry. Its first Shadow Factory-paid for and equipped by the Government but run by Rover-was ready by July 1937. And, as the international situation worsened, so Rover was asked to run a second and much larger factory, to be built on a greenfield site at Solihull, near Birmingham.

Work began on the construction of this factory in summer 1939, and by autumn the following year it was building the Bristol Hercules aero-engines which powered the Beaufighter and other aircraft then so essential to Britain's war effort. It is this very Solihull factory which today builds the Land

Rovers which figure so prominently among Britain's proudest exports.

Rover's involvement in the war effort quickly expanded, and by the end of 1942 the company was managing no fewer than 18 separate factories in the Midlands and

Rover factory, probably pictured during the 1939-45 war.

Land Rover works, Solihull, in 1990.

the North, the majority of them producing material for the Air Ministry. The manufacture of Hercules aero-engines was followed by that of Pegasus and Centaurus engine parts, by the maintenance of Cheetah aero-engines, and by the construction of airframes for the Albemarle transport and glider tug and of wings for the Lancaster bomber and for various Bristol aircraft. But perhaps the greatest tribute to Rover's abili-

ties was the Air Ministry's decision that the company should work with Frank Whittle and his team on the development of a jet aircraft engine.

Bombed out of its Coventry home in 1940, Rover eventually moved lock, stock and barrel to the Solihull Shadow Factory site; and it was there that the very first Land Rover was built in 1947. It was no surprise that this and subsequent models should have been panelled in the aircraft alloy with which Rover were by then so familiar, or that early examples should have been finished in the light green paint found in the cockpits of the wartime aircraft with whose production Rover had been so intimately involved. Nor was it very surprising when the military connection was renewed as the British Army ordered its first Land Rovers in 1948. Today, nearly half a century later, it still relies on Land Rovers-as do over a hundred more armies and paramilitary forces around the world.

From support for the Royal Air Force during those bitter years of conflict to support for peacekeeping military forces in the modern world, Solihull has a reputation for supporting the best – a reputation that today's Defenders, Discoverys and Range Rovers continue to uphold with honour.